Compliments of

Rooney,
Plotkin
& Willey,
LLP

We hope you enjoy your copy of
WealthBuilding

If you have any questions, please call
the authors at (401) 455-6707

J.K. LASSER PRO™

WEALTHBUILDING

The *J.K. Lasser Pro* Series

WealthBuilding—Investment Strategies for Retirement and Estate Planning
    David R. Reiser and Robert L. DiColo
    with Hugh M. Ryan and Andrea R. Reiser

Fee-Only Financial Planning: How to Make It Work for You
    John E. Sestina

Preparing for the Retirement Boom
    Thomas Grady

The *Wiley Financial Advisor* Series

Tax-Deferred Investing: Wealth Building and Wealth Transfer Strategies
    Cory Grant and Andrew Westhem

Getting Clients, Keeping Clients
    Dan Richards

Managing Family Trusts: Taking Control of Inherited Wealth
    Robert A. Rikoon with Larry Waschka

Advising the 60+ Investor: Tax and Financial Planning Strategies
    Darlene Smith, Dale Pulliam, and Holland Tolles

Tax-Smart Investing: Maximizing Your Client's Profits
    Andrew D. Westhem and Stewart J. Weissman

J.K. LASSER PRO™

WEALTHBUILDING

INVESTMENT STRATEGIES FOR RETIREMENT & ESTATE PLANNING

David R. Reiser, MS, CFP and
Robert L. DiColo, CLU, ChFC, CIMC
with Hugh M. Ryan and Andrea R. Reiser

John Wiley & Sons, Inc.
New York • Chichester • Weinheim • Brisbane • Singapore • Toronto

This book is printed on acid-free paper.

Copyright © 2000 by David R. Reiser, Robert L. DiColo, Hugh M. Ryan and Andrea R. Reiser. All rights reserved.

Published by John Wiley & Sons, Inc.

Published simultaneously in Canada.

J.K. Lasser Pro is a trademark of John Wiley & Sons, Inc.

To order books or for customer service call
1-800-CALL-WILEY(225-5945).

This publication is designed to provide accurate and authoritative information in regard to the subject matter covered. It is sold with the understanding that the publisher is not engaged in rendering professional services. If professional advice or other expert assistance is required, the services of a competent professional person should be sought.

Library of Congress Cataloging-in-Publication Data:

Reiser, David R.
    WealthBuilding : investment strategies for retirement and estate planning / David R.
    Reiser, Robert L. DiColo, with Hugh M. Ryan and Andrea R. Reiser.
        p. cm. — (The J.K. Lasser pro series)
    ISBN 0-471-38807-6 (cloth : alk. paper)
        1. Finance, Personal. 2. Retirement income—Planning. 3. Estate planning.
I. Title: At head of title: J.K. Lasser pro. II. DiColo, Robert L. III. Title. IV. Series.

HG179 .R386 2000
332.024'01—dc21   00-043588

Printed in the United States of America

10 9 8 7 6 5 4 3 2 1

Contents

Part Three: Preserving Wealth

Quick Guide to Wealth Stories

Name/Marital Status	Age	Employment Status	Income & Source*
Harry and Janice Greenberg, Inc. (Married couple)	60	Semiretired	$100,000 (s)
Kathleen O'Hara, Inc. (Divorced female)	52	Not employed	$120,000 (a)
Andrew and Hortense MacTavish, Inc. (Married couple)	60s	Retired	$75,000 (r)
Greg Hoessfield, Un-Inc. (Married male)	32	Employed	$100,000 (s)
James and Karen Starter, Inc. (Married couple)	29 & 28	Both employed	$60,000 (s)
George Lasaud, Inc. (Married male)	61	Employed	$100,000 (s)
Harry Nicolopolos, Inc. (Widower)	65	Newly retired	$30,000 (r)
June Washington, Inc. (Widow)	63	Retired	Commensurate with expenses
Phillip and Carol Vitale, Inc. (Married couple)	40	Both employed	Commensurate with expenses
Jack Infante, Inc. (Married male)	54	Employed	Commensurate with expenses
Francis Charlton, Inc. (Married male)	52	Employed	Commensurate with expenses
Angelo and Gina Orsini, Inc. (Married couple)	47 and 50	Both employed	Commensurate with expenses
Dr. Steven Kuchinski, Inc. (Single male)	45	Employed	$250,000 (s)

*Abbreviations: (s) = salary; (a) = alimony; (r) = retirement income; (i) = investment income

Investable Assets	Goal(s)	Obstacle	Page
$200,000	Retirement in 2 years	No Chief Operating Officer to oversee finances	*13*
$1 million	Financial comfort and independence	Unprepared to manage finances	*15*
$1.8 million	Extra luxuries in retirement	Invested too heavily in bonds	*19*
$40,000	1. Fund mortgage payments; 2. Fund kids' education; 3. Retirement	Incapable of saving	*25*
$0	1. Fund kids' education; 2. Early retirement	No savings goals or strategy	*27*
$500,000	Retirement in 3 years with European travel	Retirement savings without a retirement plan	*33*
$170,000	1. Self-sufficient retirement with a new car every 2 years; 2. Reduce federal income tax	Ineffective use of tax-advantage investments	*37*
$775,000	1. Home renovation; 2. Travel	Investment strategy excludes hedge against inflation	*38*
$100,000	1. Fund kids' education	No portfolio diversification	*54*
$340,000	Retirement in 8 to 10 years	Invested without professional advice	*62*
$175,000	Retirement in 10 years	No investment plan and a get-rich-quick mentality	*66*
$225,000	1. Comfortable retirement; 2. Help fund grandchildren's education; 3. Support charities	Traded options without knowledgeable advice	*68*
$300,000	Retirement	Invested in get-rich-quick schemes, unable to stick with investment plan	*70*

Name/Marital Status	Age	Employment Status	Income & Source*
Laura Wheelwright, Inc. (Widow)	62	Not employed	$38,400 (r)
Fred and Susan Baxter, Inc. (Married couple)	62 and 59	Fred: retired Susan: P/T	$115,000 (r)
Roger and Hazel Fonseca, Inc. (Married couple)	62 and 61	About to retire	Commensurate with expenses
Nina Lambert, Inc. (Widow)	60	Retired	$21,000 (r)
Irwin and Elaine Pollack, Inc. (Married couple)	72 and 70	Retired	$48,000+ (r)
Virginia Sewell, Inc. (Widow)	65	Newly retired	$24,000 (r, i)
Allyson Lindsay, Inc. (Single female)	24	Employed	$60,000 (s)
Diana Marsh and Ian McGillivray, Inc. (Married couple)	30s	Both employed	$350,000 (s)
Gordon and Iris Little, Inc. (Married couple)	both 60	Retired	Commensurate with expenses
Patrick and Irene Knight, Inc. (Married couple)	both 70s	Retired	Commensurate with expenses
Ken Yoshimura, Inc. (Remarried male)	64	Retired	Well beyond expenses
Wilbur and Alice Morgan, Inc. (Married couple)	both 69	Retired	Commensurate with expenses
Dr. and Mrs. Henry Bradstreet, Inc. (Married couple)	64	Employed	$100,000 (s)
The Donaldson Family, Inc. (Family)	Parents: 60s Children: 30s	Retired Employed	$100,000 (r, i)

*Abbreviations: (s) = salary; (a)= alimony; (r) = retirement income; (i) = investment income

Investable Assets	Goal(s)	Obstacle	Page
$350,000	1. Steady income; 2. Appreciation on assets	Investments scattered among several financial advisors	*78*
$1 million	1. International travel; 2. Leave substantial bequest to children	Investment strategy was for income instead of growth	*83*
$360,000	1. Home remodeling; 2. Travel; 3. Give monetary gifts to grandchildren	No comprehensive investment plan	*92*
$450,000	Increased income	Decreasing portfolio value with need for higher income	*103*
$630,000	1. Income; 2. Preservation of assets	Inadvisably invested in junk bonds and limited partnerships for income	*106*
$350,000	Comfortable retirement	No investment plan	*116*
$4,000	Financial ability to work part-time in 10 years	No savings plan or strategy	*119*
$1 million	Financial independence without employment income	No investment plan	*122*
$1.5 million (estate value)	Develop and execute estate plan	No estate plan	*135*
$400,000	Develop and execute estate plan to benefit family and charities	No estate plan	*137*
$3 million (estate value)	Comfortable retirement	Afraid to develop and execute estate plan	*139*
$480,000	Leave a substantial bequest to children and grandchildren	Fear of asset depletion in later years due to nursing care expenses	*148*
$550,000	Be a millionaire	Portfolio not structured for growth, needed encouragement to spend money	*154*
$1.25 million	Avoid heavy estate taxation; educate children about estate plan	No estate plan	*166*

Name/Marital Status	Age	Employment Status	Income & Source*
The Worthington Family, Inc. (Family)	Parents: 40s Children: 20s	Employed Students	Beyond expenses
Helga van Leewen, Inc. (Widow)	65	Retired	$24,000 (r)
Louise Upton, Inc. (Single female)	70s	Retired	$20,000 (r)
Oswald and Henrietta Stone, Inc. (Married couple)	60s	Semiretired	Commensurate with expenses

*Abbreviations: (s) = salary; (a)= alimony; (r) = retirement income; (i) = investment income

Investable Assets	Goal(s)	Obstacle	Page
$1 million	Teach young adult children financial responsibility	Young adult children had no experience managing finances	*168*
$350,000	Leave a substantial charitable bequest	No knowledge of how to set up a charitable trust	*174*
$1 million	Leave $1 million after taxes to family and charities	No investment or estate plan	*177*
$1.75 million	1. Comfortable retirement; 2. Ability to pass down highly valued real estate to children without forced liquidation; 3. Fund a family gifting plan	No investment or estate plan	*183*

Acknowledgments

We extend our deepest gratitude to our writing team, Hugh Ryan and Andrea Reiser (wife of one of the authors). While we brought to the project our vast knowledge of financial information, we felt it best to take our own advice and leave the writing aspect to professionals. Hugh was introduced to us by Andrea, as they are former colleagues; she portrayed him as one of the most masterful business writers she'd ever known. Hugh was able to fathom the warp and woof of our operation, including the nature of our client relationships and service. He spent days listening to us prattle ceaselessly about technical market information, and willingly endured our countless, anxious, late-night and weekend telephone calls to him. Hugh managed to craft from our chatter excellent copy, eloquently putting our ideas and experiences into clear, concise words.

We credit Andrea with conceiving the idea for this book, encouraging us to pursue it, and managing with great skill and panache the writing, editing, design, and production to the bitter end. With creativity and tenacity, Andrea enhanced Hugh's copy by interweaving a warm, friendly nuance, capturing a writing style that we feel closely represents our voice. In addition, she provided inspired original writing, meticulous copyediting, and detailed style and layout specifications on exceedingly tight deadlines. Andrea repeatedly set aside for weeks at a time her responsibilities as President of Image Communications, a copywriting and graphic design firm—and, more importantly, sacrificed precious time as the mommy of four little boys—to lend her writing talent and design expertise to the project. We are enormously grateful to Andrea for the energy, patience, diligence, and flair that she devoted to bring *WealthBuilding* to fruition.

Debra Englander, our editor at Wiley, guided us graciously through the process that was so unfamiliar to us. She allowed us the freedom to create our vision, and we greatly appreciate her guidance and counsel.

For more than ten years, the late Robert J. Gulla was our boss and our mentor; he still remains our standard of excellence. We wish Bob were here to read these words, but he is with us in spirit.

Sincere thanks to our stellar office staff: Cathy Gibney DiColo, Sandy Smith, and Donna Laird. These talented professionals play a tremendously important role in the daily operation of our business, and their dedication to our clients allowed us to take the time we needed to put this book together.

Steve Brown, our branch manager at PaineWebber's Providence office, has been extremely supportive of us in both achieving our business objectives and writing this book. He is always willing to go to bat for us and is the consummate problem-solver.

Speaking of PaineWebber, we are pleased to be part of an organization that encourages and fosters an entrepreneurial attitude in its investment professionals. Without this freedom, we would not have been able to achieve the goals we set for ourselves during the past 14 years.

Special thanks to Bill Lytton, whose eloquent words captured the essence of the book in the Foreword. Hats off to Zoë Baird, Dr. Bob Goodman, Al Horvath, Ken Swimm, John Tarantino, and Cap Willey, who previewed the manuscript and lent their kind comments to the back cover and praise page.

John Harpootian, Esq., reviewed some of the estate planning material in the book. He and his business partner, Ben Paster, Esq., are estate planning experts who have provided to us and our clients valuable legal counsel for many years.

We are each individually grateful for the strength of our partnership. Working together since 1986, we are a classic example of a whole being much more than a sum of its parts. Our partnership has allowed each of us to grow personally and professionally throughout the years, and we truly value and admire each other's character.

Finally, we have ultimate gratitude toward our clients for entrusting us with such monumental responsibility. We are profoundly privileged and humbled to be not only their financial advisors, but also their partners in achieving their dreams and, in many cases, their friends.

D.R.R. and R.L.D.
September 2000

Foreword

By William B. Lytton

Almost everyone has heard the expression that a lawyer who represents himself has a fool for a client. Why is that? It probably reflects the reality that when you represent yourself, you lack a bit of objectivity. You assume too much or too little. You don't ask the tough questions, and other things keep interfering in your time and ability to focus on your own affairs. Lawyers, like the classic shoemaker whose children went shoeless, tend to focus on their clients first, and themselves only second.

The same applies to investing wisely for retirement or for estate planning. There is a tendency among many of us either to put it off, or to approach it in a non-professional manner. We don't need professional investment advisors. Right? After all, we are reasonably intelligent and well-informed. We read the papers. We occasionally see investment gurus on TV, and we can access the Internet and find out everything we need to know about stocks, bonds, and the performance of mutual funds. So, why would we need help?

I once went to a lecture where the speaker described a process where first we gather data, then we discern facts, which leads us to knowledge, and forms the basis for wisdom. It is a long way from data to wisdom. And while there is a great deal of free data available from a variety of sources, there is precious little free wisdom. Those who think that watching a show on investing provides the basis for a customized approach for their families probably also read the daily horoscope in the paper and believe that it carries a specific message meant for them alone. If we behaved that way, then every day all Leos and Capricorns would be acting the same—foolishly. And that is the problem with using a similarly naïve and foolish approach to planning for your own future and the needs of your family or for those other people or charitable institutions you might wish to support.

Data, facts, and even knowledge are not enough when it is the financial well-being of my family at stake. I want wisdom—or as close to it as I can get. Making wise decisions that weigh the individual needs of those involved, consider the changes in circumstances that may occur, and evaluate the variety of investment or estate planning options available should be the goal of anyone contemplating how to accumulate, live on, and distribute wealth. Even how we define wealth will vary from person to person—based upon their abilities, needs, expectations, and values.

Dave Reiser and Bob DiColo describe in this book any number of examples of the individualized attention that is essential to helping each person achieve his or her own unique goals. They approach the concept of investment strategy as if they were the Chief Operating Officers (COOs) of the private companies whose assets are the sum of each individual's abilities, savings, hopes, and plans. If you are like me, you have other things to do that prevent you from constantly thinking about running your own investment portfolio in the context of volatile markets. Most of us can benefit by having a COO worrying about the details and, within the context of the strategy and goals we set, bringing alternatives and options to us to help us achieve those goals.

You will see in the pages that follow many ways in which this point is made. Like me, you may see examples that come uncomfortably close to the quick in describing things not done, opportunities not taken, and the lure of short-term whims overwhelming longer-term strategies. The good news is that it is almost never too late to make the adjustments—mentally as well as financially—that are required. However, the longer we wait, the more opportunities are lost.

There are many fine investment advisors out there. Their interest is to help you make wise decisions. This book shows how two of those advisors have accomplished that goal for their clients, and how everyone can benefit from this type of wise, well-planned, and personalized strategic planning in their own lives.

And when you have finished reading this book, pass it along to your spouse and your adult children.

William B. Lytton is Senior Vice President and General Counsel of International Paper. He has previously served as a Federal Prosecutor in Chicago and Philadelphia, and was in private practice in Philadelphia. He also served as Deputy Special Counselor to President Ronald Reagan.

PART

1

Defining Wealth

Introduction

"The entire essence of America is the hope to first
make money—then make money with money—
then make lots of money with lots of money."

—*Paul Erdman*

"The best executive is the one who has sense enough to
pick good men to do what he wants done, and self-restraint
enough to keep from meddling with them while they do it."

—*Theodore Roosevelt*

Don't Do It Yourself

Investment advice on the Internet, television, newsletters, and other mass media provides information to individual investors quite readily—information that used to be available only through investment firms or extensive library research.

The easy availability of this information has many benefits, but it has spawned one ill-conceived idea: That investors can easily learn—in their spare time—everything that financial professionals know, thereby enabling them to take a do-it-yourself approach to investing, and saving a fortune in fees and commissions. A host of advertising and marketing programs by online stock-trading services, investment-advice newsletters, and purveyors of mutual funds and other investment vehicles explicitly promote what we consider to be this bad idea. Many pundits and journalists reinforce this notion.

We maintain that there is a difference between information and knowledge. Our book is intended to counter this do-it-yourself trend by demonstrating and illustrating a better way. We have written it with two types of readers in mind. First are serious investors with at least $100,000 to invest, who want to plan for their own and their families' futures by taking advantage of the best financial counsel and service available. We want to help you understand the principles of financial planning, and the value and methodology of working with a seasoned, highly capable financial planning and investment professional. Second are financial service professionals—accountants, lawyers, insurance agents, and others to whom people turn for investment, tax, and estate planning advice. This book is intended to guide you in helping your clients define and achieve wealth.

Each chapter includes information that will benefit both types of readers. The chapters end with a more technical section titled, "Professional's Toolkit" designed to address specific issues that are relevant to financial service professionals. Individual investors may choose to read these sections as well, although the information is not necessary to gain a full understanding of the process described in the book.

How Can an Idea So Popular Be So Wrong?

Why do we argue that individual investors should not be encouraged to go it alone? Because there is a distinct difference and an enormous gap in knowledge between a person who has read a stack of reports on a topic and an expert professional in that field. If you have earned and saved at least $100,000 to invest for retirement, you have obviously developed abilities in your chosen career field, whether it's sales, medicine, teaching, engineering, architecture, or another business or profession. Your financial advisor cannot acquire your professional skills simply by downloading information from the Internet. Likewise, you cannot acquire an educated, competent financial advisor's knowledge of investments, taxation, and estate planning from the Internet or a fistful of newsletters and magazine articles.

A case in point is the plethora of medical information available on the Internet that helps people understand their afflictions and participate in their own treatment. They use the information to seek out leading hospitals and doctors, to connect with people who share their diseases, and to obtain the best medical care from the most qualified doctors and specialists. They do *not* substitute this information for a doctor's care.

In a similar vein, investment information from the Web and other sources can help investors weigh their options, make risk/reward judgments, determine necessary savings levels, and otherwise participate in building a sound financial future. However, we contend that, for the sake of your own financial security, you should not use the information to eliminate the professional financial advisor, but rather to enhance your prudent participation in planning your financial future.

The Right Idea

You can be certain, though, that we do not advise individual investors simply to hand their savings to a financial professional and walk away. That approach makes no more sense than the opposite extreme of investors' trying to do everything themselves. Rather, we recommend a three-step process:

Step 1. You, Inc. As a serious investor, you should approach your financial future with a novel mindset: Think of your investments and future as a virtual company and appoint yourself Chief Executive Officer (CEO) of that business. If you pause to consider it, every individual or family has the essentials of a business—income, expenses, a balance sheet (assets and liabilities), and commercial (i.e., money-earning) activity. You also have goals you want to achieve. Therefore, it makes sense for you to take control of your virtual company and act as CEO—the boss—with the attendant responsibilities and perks. You should take your virtual business as seriously as your career.

Step 2. Appoint a Chief Operating Officer. As any good CEO would do, you should select and appoint a Chief Operating Officer (COO) for the business, who reports to you, the CEO. The job of the COO is to attend to the day-to-day details of managing You, Inc., freeing you up to run your own career. Whether your COO is your financial advisor, accountant, estate lawyer, or insurance agent, that person is responsible for obtaining and providing financial expertise that will enable you to run the virtual business successfully and profitably. For that service, you will pay the COO, just as the board of directors of a public company pays its COO to run the company.

Step 3. Set reasonable goals and establish a plan. With a management team now in place, you must define reasonable goals for your 40s, 50s, 60s, and beyond, considering your earning and spending patterns. You then need to work with the COO to develop a savings and investing plan that will enable your virtual company to reach these goals.

Why do we say reasonable goals? Consider Chuck and Ellen Sutcliffe, a two-income married couple, both 40 years old. Let's say they have a household income of $100,000 and have saved $100,000 for retirement. Retiring at 45 and maintaining their lifestyle would not be a reasonable goal. As a general rule, you need to have saved 10 times your highest annual income to maintain your lifestyle in retirement. Regardless of how assiduously the Sutcliffes save and how intelligently they invest, they will not be able to add $900,000 to their investments in five years. However, retiring at 55 (rather than 62 or 65) might be a reasonable goal. For the Sutcliffes, this might constitute a wealth they can achieve. Helping this couple define wealth for themselves is one function of the COO.

The objective of this three-step process is wealth, and each individual investor or family—each CEO of his or her virtual company—has a different definition.

What Is Wealth?

To some, wealth means mansions, private jets, art collections, yachts, or even their own island get-away. To others, wealth is retiring to putter in the garden and help their adult children send the grandchildren to college. Others say wealth is working six months a year, with annual trips to their ancestors' homeland or a sunny beach. To still others, wealth is living modestly, then bequeathing a significant sum to a favorite hospital or university.

Our clients take responsibility for their saving and investing plans to achieve their idea of wealth, and we encourage you to do the same. Some of them read a good deal about investments, and some do not. But all of them rely on professional investment advice to help answer questions such as these: Should I have both equity and debt investments? What are equity and debt investments? Should I buy common stocks of blue-chip, dividend-paying corporations and utilities, or of fast-growing, emerging companies?

Should they be in U.S. or foreign companies? Under what conditions do I sell bonds and buy stocks? Should I have annuities? In short, our clients know that we live and breathe investments the way they dedicate themselves to their careers.

About the Wealth Stories

We have based this book on investment strategies and results for a number of our clients. The people in this book are not composites of several people. Each Wealth Story refers to a specific individual or family whose investments we have managed and, in most cases, still manage as the book goes to press. For the sake of our clients' privacy, we have changed their names and the incidental details that are peripheral to the investment strategy and results. But each example fairly describes a client—his or her dreams, goals, and investment history. Many of these success stories begin with the investors in the hands of the wrong financial advisors; all the stories end with the investors' having appointed themselves CEOs of their virtual companies.

PART

2

Achieving Wealth

CHAPTER

1

How to Pick the Right Chief Operating Officer

"It requires a great deal of boldness and a great deal of caution to make a great fortune, and when you have it, it requires ten times as much skill to keep it."

—*Ralph Waldo Emerson*

Getting to the Chief Operating Officer Point

For the reasons explained in the Introduction, investors who have saved $100,000 or more should seek a Chief Operating Officer (COO) for their virtual company. But how do you get to this $100,000 point? The simplest way is to participate fully in your company's 401(k) plan or similar retirement or savings program. If your company offers this benefit, enroll immediately and save, save, save! If you aren't eligible to participate in a company-sponsored retirement savings program—or, better yet, as a supplement to your existing 401(k) plan—select a conservative mutual fund with a good three-, five-, and ten-year performance record and be religious about making monthly deposits. These conservative mutual funds typically contain a diversity of **blue-chip stocks** and other fixed-income instruments such as **U.S. Treasury bonds.**

Blue-chip stocks are dividend-paying common stocks of large ($5 billion or more market capitalization), well-established corporations that have been profitable over decades and have strong market positions. Examples include IBM, Ford Motor Company, Dow Chemical, General Electric, Wal-Mart, and Bristol-Myers.

U.S. Treasury bonds are marketable, fixed-interest U.S. government debt securities with maturity of more than 10 years. All U.S. Treasury instruments are backed by the full faith and credit of the federal government.

Once you reach the point where you need a COO for your virtual company, hiring that person will be the most important decision you will make in securing your financial future. Yet, believe it or not, many people spend more time and energy, and do more research before selecting a new car than they do before identifying a person to help manage everything they own.

Who Makes a Good Financial Advisor?

Whether the financial advisor is the COO or a specialized team member of You, Inc., the advisor should work for a major national or international investment firm. This is not because large firms have a monopoly on intelligence or experience; they don't. The reason to select a national investment firm is its resources. No single person or small group can read everything or know everything. Investment advisors at large firms have staff economists, investment strategists, and technical analysts who constantly feed them relevant information. Investment advisors at large firms have business relationships, service offices, and access to the leading money managers nationwide. These firms hold their top performers to strict standards of ethics and provide a level of oversight that, we believe, small firms cannot match. In other words, we are convinced that the large firms offer an assurance and an insurance—safety—that small, independent firms do not.

Good financial advisors operate on the basis of a soundly researched view of U.S. and global investment markets for the coming five years. They constantly update that understanding and check it against market activity every year. The financial planner's global view takes into account corporate earnings, interest rates, inflation, budget and trade surpluses and deficits, and the overall health of the U.S. and global economy.

Choosing a financial advisor from a large national or international investment firm ensures a global view that is not only the financial advisor's personal opinion. Rather, it should reflect the intelligence and analysis of the firm as well.

In addition, you and the prospective financial advisor need to be candid and thorough in exchanging information at your first meeting. We have detailed the information that both parties should bring to an introductory meeting in Appendices A, B, and C.

But I'm a Person, Not a Company!

Encouraging investors to regard themselves as virtual companies is not meant to dehumanize them—in fact, the intent is just the opposite. We urge our clients to plan their futures and take the necessary actions to fulfill their dreams with the organization, analysis, and dispassionate allocation of resources that CEOs use to drive successful corporations. We urge our clients to view themselves as the CEO, who sets the goals and the timetables. Many times we then become the COO who helps make it all happen.

We help our clients achieve their life goals—wealth as they define it.

□ □ □

Harry and Janice Greenberg, Inc.

Harry and Janice Greenberg were earning an excellent income (more than $100,000 per year) and using the advice of several financial professionals—a stockbroker, an insurance agent, an accountant, and a lawyer. Yet, they were setting themselves up for financial worry, strain, and deprivation in what should have been their leisure years. Why? Because they were not viewing their family finances like a business, had no long-range plan, and had no single, trusted financial professional (no COO) to oversee their earning, saving, spending, and investing.

The Greenbergs' stockbroker would call periodically with hot tips—stocks he said were bound to gain substantial value soon. Occasionally, he was right; more often he was wrong. The accountant prepared their tax returns. The insurance agent made sure Janice was provided for should Harry die prematurely, and the lawyer had drawn up and executed a standard will.

Yet while most of these professionals had delivered their particular service acceptably, none of them had taken a comprehensive look at the Greenbergs' goals, assets, and spending patterns. In 1989, tired of losing money and with Harry's sixtieth birthday approaching, the Greenbergs assessed their financial situation. They quickly realized that without having saved prudently and purposefully during the previous 30 years, they were in no position to retire within the foreseeable future. They took control of their situation, formed Harry and Janice Greenberg, Inc., and hired us as COO.

At that time, they had saved about $200,000 for retirement and had been looking forward to Harry's ending his career as a structural engineering consultant at age 62. They thought of $200,000 as a lot of money, which it was, but they did not realize that it would not sustain their customary lifestyle after Harry stopped working. As stated earlier, a family should save 10 times its highest annual income for retirement. Basic arithmetic shows that the Greenbergs had amassed about one-fifth of the $1 million necessary for the retirement they sought.

As COO, it was our unpleasant task to deliver a bitter pill: Harry would have to work full time until at least age 65—and part-time until at least age 70—so he and Janice could live on his income, not draw down from the $200,000, and allow **compound interest rates** to build the $200,000. We showed Harry and Janice a long-range plan built on this foundation that would provide the needed $1 million by the time they reached age 70. Even though the plan called for Harry's complete retirement eight to ten years later than they had hoped for, the Greenbergs were enthusiastic. For the first time, they had a specific financial and lifestyle goal and a plan to reach it.

Humorously called the eighth wonder of the world or Einstein's greatest discovery, **compound interest** refers to the way savings grow in value when left untouched. Invest $2,000 for 30 years at 10%, tax-deferred, and you will accumulate $34,898. Add $2,000 per year, and you will save $363,886.

We immediately consolidated the Greenbergs' $200,000, which was scattered over dozens of stocks, many of which were declining in value and a few of which were in free fall. We reinvested the savings in a combination of private money manager accounts and tax-deferred annuities. Since Harry was working full time, placing him in the highest income tax bracket, the tax deferral was important. Because of health, age difference, and the life expectancy of women versus men, the Greenbergs expected Janice to outlive Harry by 15 to 20 years. The annuities would provide income for her after his death.

From 1990 through 1993, the Greenbergs drew nothing from the $200,000. Beginning in 1994, they drew $1,000 per month, and by year's end, even with the withdrawals, the $200,000 had appreciated to $450,000. At this point, we told Harry that, as the CEO, he could cut back on his schedule but still had to work part time, increasing the drawdown from the portfolio to compensate for lost income.

By 1999, the portfolio had grown to $1 million and we were able to increase the Greenbergs' draw to nearly $1,000 per week. As this book goes to press, they are living on the $50,000 per year that they draw from the portfolio, Harry's $14,000 annual Social Security payments, Janice's $6,000 Social Security payments, and the $24,000 he continues to earn with a low-pressure, low-demand consulting practice. This permits Harry to work just a few hours per week and enjoy most of his time on the golf course with Janice or playing with the grandchildren. Harry and Janice Greenberg, Inc. is a prosperous virtual company, and the two-person CEO team has achieved wealth.

Lesson: Don't wait until age 60 to have a plan. By age 50, you should be operating your virtual company, guided by its business plan. Age 40 is even better. The sooner you establish your virtual company and appoint a COO, the sooner you can begin working together to build and execute a realistic plan to reach your goals.

Kathleen O'Hara, Inc.

In 1995, Kathleen O'Hara of Boston faced as desperate and extreme a need to adopt a businesslike approach to her finances as any client we have ever had. Fifty-two years old at the time, her 30-year marriage to a wealthy, high-tech entrepreneur was disintegrating. Furthermore, the marriage had not prepared her to manage her finances.

Her husband's commercial success had funded a luxurious lifestyle and relieved Kathleen of the need to plan or budget, to build a career, or to develop marketable skills and credentials. She had learned to spend money. If she wanted jewelry or clothing, she bought it. An avid golfer and tennis player, Kathleen would flee Massachusetts winters for resorts or spas in Arizona or the Caribbean. She never considered making herself a sandwich for lunch, instead eating at the country club or a fancy restaurant every day. She had two imported, high-ticket automobiles, a luxury sedan and a sports car.

The divorce was more amicable than most, and her husband, Sean, was a generous man. As a result, she received substantial alimony for 10 years, a $1 million cash payment, and their primary residence in a wealthy Boston suburb. As a millionaire, Kathleen did not realize that she now had to invest and manage her money expertly. Only 52 years old, she could easily outlive even this substantial divorce settlement. Indeed, with her customary spending patterns, she *would* outlive it.

So, Kathleen's challenge was not poverty or deprivation. Far from it. Even after the divorce, she had more money than most. Her challenge was twofold. (1) While she had more money than most, she had a good deal less than she had been accustomed to living on. (2) She had never had to think about money—to plan, to budget, or to live within her means. Now, at age 52, she had to limit the fulfillment of her wants, if not her needs.

It was Kathleen's long-time accountant who realized she needed to form Kathleen O'Hara, Inc., hire a COO, and include a competent financial advisor on the corporate team. That accountant became her COO and set about, as his first responsibility, clarifying the CEO's financial position to her. He pointed out that, if she invested and managed her money wisely, she need never suffer deprivation. He also pointed out that her free-spending days were over; no more flying to the Caribbean just because a cold snap had gripped New England.

"But I have $1 million," Kathleen argued. The COO responded that, if she spent 5% a year, her portfolio should grow. However, drawing five percent from $1 million would produce an annual income of $50,000, and she was accustomed to spending at a considerably higher rate.

"When the investment markets have a strong year, and your portfolio does well, you will be able to take an extra trip," he said. "In years when the market is flat, you'll have to cut back. No more luxury vacations on a whim."

Having administered a dose of merciless reality, the COO asked us, as financial advisors, to structure Kathleen's investments for maximum safety and return. We split the $1 million cash settlement between tax-deferred savings (40%) that she would not touch for at least 10 years, and a **liquid** account (60%) that she would spend down to supplement alimony.

> **Liquid assets** can be readily converted to cash, such as money in a savings account or, in Kathleen's case, corporate common stock for which an active market exists.

We invested the $400,000 tax-deferred portion in **variable annuities,** which provide compound growth, three-times tax deferred. This means that the principal compounds tax-free, the interest it earns accumulates tax-free, and the money that you would otherwise have paid in taxes compounds as well. To gain these triple tax benefits, the investor relinquishes access to the funds. Usually considered a shortcoming, this lack of access was actually a benefit in this case, because it prevented Kathleen from spending money she could not afford to dissipate.

> **Variable annuities** are contracts issued by insurance companies, purchased either lump sum or by installments. They feature an investment in an underlying portfolio of debt securities, like bonds, and equity securities, like corporate common stocks. They are called "variable" because the underlying value of the investments in the contract fluctuates over time.

The power of the three-times tax deferral is illustrated by the annuity's growth. With an average annual appreciation of 12%, Kathleen's $400,000 would triple to $1.2 million in 10 years. This was the point at which her alimony was scheduled to expire, and the age when she would become eligible for Social Security. She could then start drawing 5% from the $1.2 million annually, adding to her Social Security payments an income stream of $60,000 per year

($5,000 per month). The portfolio should then continue to grow faster than she would spend it.

For immediate living expenses, beyond what the alimony would provide, we invested the $600,000 in **large-cap** and **mid-cap domestic equities.** From this portion of her portfolio, Kathleen drew about $30,000 (5% of the total) per year to supplement the alimony. Assuming long-term annual appreciation of 10% to 12%, this portion of her portfolio has the potential to exceed $1 million by the time Kathleen's alimony runs out. If the market remains strong, she may be able to withdraw more than the 5% per year that, as this book goes to press, we anticipate.

> **Large-cap** (capitalization) and **mid-cap equities** refer to the common stocks of large and mid-sized corporations. A corporation's capitalization, or total market value, equals the number of shares of stock outstanding multiplied by the price per share. The definitions of large, mid-sized, and small-cap equities are not precise. In general, a small-cap stock has a capitalization of less than $1 billion, a mid-cap ranges from $1 billion to $5 billion, and a large cap exceeds $5 billion.

Now five years into the investment plan for Kathleen O'Hara, Inc., the CEO enjoys a lifestyle that is more modest than that of her married years, but one that affords her independence, security, and a reasonable number of luxuries. She also has an investment plan. Until age 62, Kathleen will live on the alimony and the $600,000 of the $1 million cash payment that is invested in liquid assets. At age 62, she will start to draw on the $400,000 that will have been appreciating untouched for 10 years, using those withdrawals to replace the alimony. Social Security will begin at that time as well.

Lesson: Do not depend on your spouse or anyone else to earn, manage, and invest all the family's money, because death or divorce can remove that person suddenly and without warning. Even if you are not the breadwinner, help the breadwinner budget, save, and invest for the future. Someday, you may need that knowledge.

Select a COO whom you trust and who can bring to the team equally skilled and trustworthy financial colleagues.

Andrew and Hortense MacTavish, Inc.

The MacTavishes came to us in 1994, when Andrew was 62 and Hortense 61, dissatisfied with their financial advisor. Based on frugality and Andrew's distinguished career as a research chemist for a large, multinational pharmaceutical company, they had amassed nearly $2 million in investments and almost $1 million in real estate surrounding their rural Connecticut home.

After attending a seminar we gave, they followed the self-examination and analysis processes outlined in the three tear-out appendices at the back of this book. The MacTavishes were quite specific about the characteristics a new financial advisor/COO would need to possess in order to join their virtual company. At our first meeting, they quizzed us relentlessly about our experience, education, and investment philosophy. They also freely provided the necessary information about themselves.

The process revealed that, although they enjoyed a substantial pension and Social Security, which provided for all their living expenses, they had $650,000 of their $1.8 million portfolio in government and blue-chip corporate bonds. Their previous financial advisor had relied on generic, cookie-cutter, pseudo-analysis to devise their investment strategy. He said, "You're retired. You should be in safe bonds to provide a steady, reliable income. Stocks are too risky for retired folks."

The problem is not that such thinking is always unintelligent. Often, **investment-grade bonds** are the best vehicle for retired people—especially if their own investments generate most or all of their income. The problem is that the analysis is generic, not tailored to the specific situation of the client at hand.

> **Investment-grade bonds** are bonds that are assigned a rating in the top four categories by commercial credit rating companies. Standard & Poor's classifies investment-grade bonds as BBB or higher, and Moody's classifies them as Ba or higher. By contrast, high-yield bonds carry a credit rating from S&P of BB or lower, or a Moody's rating of Ba or lower.

A closer look at the MacTavishes' situation and frank input from the couple revealed that this formula had overlooked one crucial factor: With a pension and Social Security providing necessary living expenses, they did not need steady, safe income from their investments. They actually could afford the limited risk of investing in stocks of blue-chip companies to benefit from the superior growth that these stocks provide versus investment-grade bonds. Furthermore, they were paying significant income tax on the interest payments generated by the bonds. If instead the MacTavishes invested that money in stocks and subsequently encountered a need for more income, they could sell off shares and would pay 20% capital gains tax on any shares held for over a year, a far lower tax rate than the income tax bracket where their affluence placed them.

The MacTavishes had told their previous investment advisor repeatedly that they felt secure with their pension and Social Security and wanted to participate in the stock market. He had neglected to listen to the CEOs of Andrew and Hortense MacTavish, Inc., and after several frustrating years, the MacTavishes began their search for a COO who would consider their unique situation in developing a financial plan.

As their new COO, we worked with them to strategize using the pension and Social Security for income and reinvesting $650,000 from government bonds into blue-chip common stocks. By late 1999, that portion of their portfolio had appreciated to $1.5 million, providing their one prized luxury, an extended European vacation every summer.

Lesson: Remember this adage: "No generalization is true 100% of the time, including this one." The relevance of this saying to our discussion is that, by definition, cookie-cutter (often, nowadays, computer-generated) investment formulas cannot take into account the personal circumstances and goals of a real individual or family. You need to be sure that your COO listens to you and confident that he or she sets you on the right path for achieving your definition of wealth.

Lessons of Chapter 1

The stewardship of the money that any person or family earns is as important to their long-term security, happiness, and wealth as the earning of it. That stewardship requires a thoughtful, attentive approach—equal in seriousness to the effort devoted to the career(s) that produced the assets—and the advice of a financial advisor or advisory team. That individual or team must offer investment, tax, and inheritance expertise.

■ ■ ■

Professional's Toolkit

Becoming a COO for Your Clients

If one of your clients approaches you about serving as COO because you have earned the client's trust as accountant, lawyer, or insurance agent, you should ask yourself the following questions: Can I function as my client's COO, bringing into the virtual company a professional financial planner—someone who knows investments as well as I know balance sheets, taxation, or insurance? Or, should my client appoint a financial planner as COO and retain me to continue to provide the financial service (whether it's accounting, estate planning, or insurance) that I have been providing?

Both approaches work. In some cases, the financial planner is the COO, calling in lawyers, accountants, insurance experts, and others as needed. In other cases, one of these other specialists will be the COO, turning to the financial planner strictly for investment advice.

Which route should you follow? That depends on such factors as how broad your knowledge is of tax law, investments, estate law, and insurance; how familiar you are with Modern Portfolio Theory; and how much trust the client places in you.

For more information about the issues and information to include at an introductory meeting with a prospective client, see Appendices A, B, and C, the tear-out sections at the back of this book.

CHAPTER 2

Pitfall 1:
Don't Save During
Prime Earning Years

"Every morning, I get up and look through the Forbes list of the
richest people in America. If I'm not there, I go to work."
—*Robert Orben*

"If you don't want to work, you have to work to earn enough
money so that you won't have to work."
—*Ogden Nash*

The Importance of Saving From an Early Age

"I cannot save for retirement. It's all I can do to meet expenses. I
just don't make enough money to put anything aside for the future."

Financial professionals hear statements like this all the time, if, in
fact, they can get their clients to talk with them about retirement at all.
And believe it or not, just like the fabled cobbler's shoeless children,
many financial professionals themselves make the same excuses.

The truth is quite different. Virtually all of us can—and must—
save for retirement during our early-career and prime earning years.

Are there exceptions? Yes, rare ones. A few lucky people make
enough money, or have enough self-discipline, to save for retirement
effortlessly. A few unlucky people are beset by medical problems or
other circumstances that make it literally impossible for them to
save. When this is true, it is usually for a relatively short period.

We believe that a crucial role of any financial professional—CPA,
tax or estate lawyer, banker, insurance agent, or stockbroker—is to get

clients to face the truth: Unless you win the lottery or manage to buy the next Microsoft or Wal-Mart **IPO** or some other **hot issue,** it will be tough—and it will seem impossible—to save for retirement. But it is necessary. There is hardly any point in this book more important than this one.

Initial Public Offering (IPO) is the first time that common stock in a corporation is traded on the open market and is, therefore, available to the general public.

Hot issue is often used loosely to refer to a stock that generates a great deal of interest and following. Used precisely and accurately, the term refers to a National Association of Securities Dealers (NASD) definition. That definition is a Securities and Exchange Commission-registered public offering with an over-the-counter bid that is higher than the fixed public offering price on the day the security is first offered for sale. Special rules apply to the underwriting syndicate's distribution of such securities.

People often look ahead to an expected bonus, proceeds of a real estate sale, or another lump-sum infusion of cash, and promise themselves and their financial professionals, "We'll put that aside for retirement." Then, when the money comes, and the taxes are paid, something inevitably pops up—a vacation, continuing-ed college courses, an unexpected auto or home repair, or maybe even a wedding. "Well, that takes care of this year's bonus," they say. "We'll save next year's." The trouble is, next year may or may not bring another annual bonus, but it will certainly bring another excuse to spend rather than save.

We document to our clients that, the longer you wait, the more you must save to accumulate the amount you decide you will need at age 60 or 70. Consider these daunting facts:

To create a $1 million retirement nest egg for age 65, with 12% compound total annual return on your savings, you must save and invest the following amounts:

$85 per month, if you start at age 25.
$285 per month, if you start at age 35.
$1,000 per month, if you start at age 45.
$4,300 per month, if you start at age 55.

As you can see, being a retired millionaire at age 65 is a reasonable goal, if you start saving when you are young and save consistently. It becomes more and more difficult the older you grow and the later you start.

Clients have said to us, "But I don't have an ambition to be a millionaire. I just want to be comfortable." We point out that, to maintain their working-years lifestyle in retirement, they should save 10 times their highest annual salary. So, those who say that they don't want to be a millionaire, are essentially saying that they do not expect their household income (two or more full time salaries, for many families) to reach $100,000.

Following are two Wealth Stories of acquaintances and clients who, when they met us, said they could not save for retirement. One has listened to us for 10 years and is glad he did. One just started listening to us. We don't know if he has yet figured out that he should have listened to us 10 years ago, but, if he doesn't know it yet, he surely will.

□ □ □

Greg Hoessfield—Unincorporated

Greg Hoessfield makes a good living as a real estate developer—an excellent living, in fact. A business colleague of Greg's referred us to him in 1990 when he was 32 and already earning $100,000 annually. To complement his $100,000 salary and bonus, however, he had zero savings. This situation was especially absurd because his employer had a **defined-benefit plan** and a **401(k) plan.**

A **defined-benefit plan,** as the name implies, specifies the retiree's benefits at the time of enrollment. Such plans contrast with "defined-contribution" plans, such as the one described below.

401(k) plans are defined-contribution retirement plans maintained by employers and employee organizations, such as labor unions. They allow employees to defer receipt of income, and therefore taxation on it, until their employment ends, or even later. They are called "defined contribution" because the employee's and, in some cases, the employer's contributions are specified at enrollment. Benefits, however, are not specified and depend on the amount contributed and the return earned by the plan's investments.

Choosing not to participate in the 401(k) plan, Greg was squandering an enviable salary and irresponsibly ignoring the long-term needs of his wife and children. He was also sacrificing the money that his employer was more than willing to contribute to his financial stability, since the company contributed 50 cents for every dollar an employee invested in the 401(k). Greg had managed to accumulate $60,000 in his defined-benefit plan account, but he then borrowed $20,000 against it for the down payment on a home.

We argued. We pleaded. We virtually begged Greg to start a regular savings plan. We used logic, reason, and emotion. We appealed to love; we appealed to avarice. Greg would not budge. Finally, we outlined his three alternatives:

1. Count on working until the day you die, and buy a $2 million term life insurance policy for your wife, in case you die young.

2. Sell your home, replace it with one that is substantially less expensive, invest every marginal dollar you earn on the sale, and save the difference in the mortgage payments every month, without fail.

3. Find a new job with a substantially higher salary, and save every cent of the difference between it and your current salary.

Greg's solution was to do nothing. We met with Greg's colleague who referred him to us twice annually, at least, because this colleague had formed a virtual company and appointed us COO to oversee his investments and manage his retirement plan. Often, we met in the offices where he and Greg worked, so we would meet with Greg too. We spoke bluntly, heart-to-heart with him, and he plainly did not want to face the truth.

Greg adamantly refused to save. He persisted in hoping for a miracle—the lottery, the hot IPO (we never figured out how he thought he would identify the next Microsoft before everyone else), or the biggest sale of his career. We left each meeting shaking our heads in bewilderment.

Finally, in 1997, after several years of fearing that Greg would shoot the messenger (us), we made progress. With his employer's help, we induced Greg to enroll in the 401(k) plan, saving 3% of his salary (half what he could have saved). At this time, the employer disbanded the defined-benefit pension plan, replacing it with a profit-sharing plan. Greg used the tax-free distribution from the pension plan to pay off the loan he had taken against it. We thought we had turned a corner with Greg until we learned that he had received a $10,000 raise that year and had spent every dime.

The next year, Greg left the real estate development firm and established a company in the same business with three long-time rivals. All four are highly capable real estate professionals, and their firm is prospering. In the first year of the firm's existence, Greg doubled his salary. We were unable to persuade him to save the entire difference, as he should have, but he at least contributes the maximum to the 401(k) plan. He also makes double payments on his mortgage twice annually in order to pay it off earlier. This way, he and his wife will own the home when he reaches retirement age—even if he cannot retire then. He has also purchased a $500,000 term life insurance policy on himself payable to his three children, in addition to the $2 million policy payable to his wife.

As 1999 came to a close, Greg, at age 42, did not enjoy the secure, affluent future that his career success would have provided, given a minimum amount of self-discipline. Had he started investing the 6% maximum in his 401(k) plan when we met him 10 years ago, he would have had more than $1 million at retirement assuming a modest 8% compounded rate of return. Instead, the 10-year delay in investing will provide him just over $400,000 at age 62, with the same 8% return. That is part of what Greg has cost himself and his family.

Lesson: Start saving when you are young, or work until you die—hoping and praying that your health permits.

James and Karen Starter, Inc.

One of us met James Starter in 1988 while vacationing in the Pacific Northwest. Twenty-nine at the time, James managed a sporting goods store where I stopped for fishing gear for my annual pursuit of Skagit River salmon. A local native, James provided invaluable advice on scenic and productive fishing areas, as well as local restaurants—the part of the vacation my wife enjoyed most. He was a gregarious guy, little younger than I, and I liked him instantly.

On our last night in Washington State, my wife and I invited James and his wife to dinner to thank him for his hospitality and fishing advice. The conversation turned to saving and investing when James asked that recurrent question: "Got any hot stock tips?"

"That depends on your investment objectives," I replied and soon found that James and his wife, Karen, were not saving for the future at all—not for their children's college, let alone retirement.

"We just cannot seem to put any money away," said Karen. "We try."

As store manager, James was earning about $32,000 annually, and Karen made nearly as much as a dental technician. Karen's mother cared for their two young daughters while James and Karen worked. They had a household income of $60,000, had no day-care expenses, and were not foolishly self-indulgent. In addition, both James' and Karen's employers offered 401(k) plans. The sporting goods store matched their employees' contributions dollar for dollar, and the dentist contributed 50 cents on the dollar. As neither participated, I pointed out that they were sacrificing $1.50 that their employers were willing to invest in their retirement for every $2 they invested. If they saved 6% of their $60,000 annual gross earnings, their account balance would increase not by $3,600 per year, but by $6,360. And those figures were just contributions, not including appreciation. In short, the Starters had no excuse not to begin saving, as the following chart shows.

	Annual Salary	6% Contribution	Employer's Match	Total Contribution
James	$32,000	$1,920	$1,920	$3,840
Karen	$28,000	$1,680	$ 840	$2,520
TOTALS	$60,000	$3,600	$2,760	$6,360

That first discussion sparked something in the Starters. Back at home the next week, I received a call from James. He and Karen had both enrolled in their 401(k) plans, saving 3% of salary. It was a beginning, and in 1989, both James and Karen increased their 401(k) plan contributions to the maximum allowed 6%.

Over the years, both authors became long-distance friends and advisors to the Starters. In 1992, James earned a promotion to regional manager of several of his employer's retail locations, with a raise to $75,000 per year and options on 5,000 shares of company stock. The Starters asked if we thought they could afford for Karen to quit work and be a full time homemaker, since James' new salary was slightly more than their combined 1991 income.

We said, yes, if they would save for retirement in addition to their 401(k) plan. It was a struggle, but the Starters agreed. James invested $5,000 in a high-technology mutual fund and they agreed to add $1,000 per month to it. To foster their self-discipline, we started mailing mock invoices for $1,000 every month, which the Starters treated like a monthly bill, and paid to themselves. After seven years, the Starters have amassed $175,000 in that mutual fund.

And the story gets better. In 1999, James accepted a position as Midwest Regional Manager of a competing chain, with a base salary of $175,000 and an annual incentive bonus of $25,000. The new position is based in Austin, Texas. The Starters sold their home in Washington for $150,000, and used the equity for a down payment on a $500,000 home outside Austin. James' parents had bought the Washington house for $35,000 in 1965, and given it to James and Karen when they retired to Arizona.

James exercised his stock options at the Pacific Northwest employer for $500,000. Since it was a nonqualified stock option program, the Starters pocketed just under $250,000 after taxes. As we enter the year 2000, the Starters are well positioned financially for the future, as shown in Fig. 2.1. They have formed James & Karen Starter, Inc., with college education for the girls and an early retirement for James as their definition of wealth. As COOs, we will help them achieve that reasonable goal.

1988		1999
$60,000	Household Income	$200,000
$100,000	Residence Value	$500,000
$0	Retirement Savings Portfolio	$625,000*

*This consists of $175,000 invested in the technology mutual fund, $250,000 in a private asset money management account, and $200,000 in James' current employer's 401(k) plan.

FIGURE 2.1 The Starters' Financial Position

Lesson: Start saving young. You can do it, even when it seems you cannot. Remember this adage: Time in the market—not timing

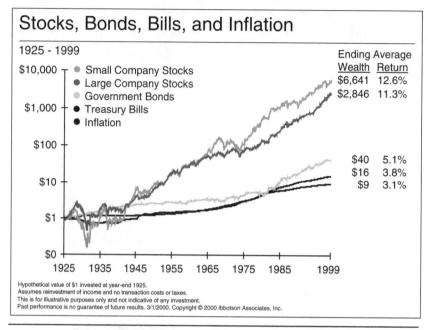

Stocks, Bonds, Bills, and Inflation

1925 - 1999

	Ending Average
	Wealth Return
● Small Company Stocks	$6,641 12.6%
● Large Company Stocks	$2,846 11.3%
Government Bonds	
● Treasury Bills	
● Inflation	

$40   5.1%
$16   3.8%
$9   3.1%

Hypothetical value of $1 invested at year-end 1925.
Assumes reinvestment of income and no transaction costs or taxes.
This is for illustrative purposes only and not indicative of any investment.
Past performance is no guarantee of future results. 3/1/2000. Copyright © 2000 Ibbotson Associates, Inc.

FIGURE 2.2 Accumulated Wealth 1925–1999

the market—is the key to success. This means that, if you invest intelligently and conservatively and stick to your investment strategy through bull and bear markets, history tells us that your investment portfolio will appreciate substantially in the long run, as you can see in Fig. 2.2. If you try to time the market, that is, outguess the market to buy low and sell high, you are gambling. Might you win? Yes, but you might also lose everything.

Lesson of Chapter 2

Saving for retirement during the early-career and prime earning years turns securing your retirement from a Mission Impossible into a highly manageable task. Younger investors should look at it this way: Would you rather work hard, scrimp, and sacrifice during your younger, healthier years, and then be free to spend most of your higher salary in middle age? Or, would you rather defer saving, then have to labor and deny yourself through middle age into your later years, when your friends are retiring?

■ ■ ■

Professional's Toolkit

Rolling Over Retirement Plan Distributions

During your clients' prime earning years, they are likely to change jobs and receive distributions from their employers' 401(k) or other deferred-taxation plans. There are other conditions under which your clients may receive a distribution, such as changes in retirement benefits by their employers. In these cases, it is important to ensure that they are aware of the need to roll over their distributions directly into eligible retirement plans such as an Individual Retirement Account (IRA) or their new employer's plan. This will avoid immediate and otherwise-unnecessary tax obligations.

Many people do not understand that, if they accept a lump-sum distribution when they leave a deferred-tax plan, their employer will automatically withhold 20% of that distribution and send it to the IRS for credit against that year's income tax. In addition, if your client is under 59½ years of age, he or she will be subject to an additional 10% penalty tax for early withdrawal.

Once your client receives the distribution, the following options apply for rolling it into an eligible plan:

- Roll the 80% that the employer did not withhold within 60 days. (The 20% that the employer withheld and sent to the IRS will be considered taxable income.)

- Roll 100% of the distribution within 60 days by coming up with the cash to replace the 20% withheld, which will be credited toward the current year's income tax liability.

It is simpler to avoid the 20% employer withholding by arranging for the direct rollover. That is the course we recommend you pursue with your client.

Congress established the rollover IRA, or conduit IRA, solely for people to receive distributions from qualified plans. Your client may leave the distribution in the conduit IRA or add it to a qualified plan offered by the next employer. By leaving the money in the conduit IRA, the client can benefit from tax-deferred growth and the wide range of investment choices available for any tax-deferred plan.

If your client decides to roll over the entire distribution, make sure he or she contacts the institution where the conduit IRA will be established to obtain the necessary paperwork and instructions.

And, make sure the client instructs the former employer to make the check payable to the IRA custodian to avoid the 20% withholding.

If your client is accepting a position with a new employer who offers a qualified, tax-deferred plan, the client should ask the benefits administrator if it accepts rollover contributions. Some do and some don't. If the plan does not accept rollover contributions, your client will need to leave the distribution in the conduit IRA or another qualified IRA to defer taxation.

The rules regarding distributions are complex, with many conditions and exceptions. In all likelihood, your client will not be conversant with the rules, and you may not be either. So, you must ensure that your client confers with a banker, CPA, or other authority who can prevent unnecessary tax burdens.

Pitfall 2:
Save Blindly, without Goals or a Plan

"Save a little money each month and at the end of
the year you'll be surprised at how little you have."
—*Ernest Haskins*

"Strategic planning is worthless—
unless there is first a strategic vision."
—*John Naisbitt*

The Right Investment Mix

The previous chapter illustrated the danger of insufficient saving during prime earning years. But saving, while necessary, is not sufficient. It is equally important to put in place the proper combination of investment instruments, selecting those that are most appropriate and effective in achieving your financial needs and life goals.

□ □ □

George Lasaud, Inc.

George Lasaud forged a successful management and executive career with a Fortune 500 corporation in the industrial rust belt of upstate New York after graduating from college in 1950. In 1990, at age 61, he decided to review his substantial, career-long savings with an eye to retirement in three years. Executive responsibility during the final several years of George's career earned him an annual salary of about $100,000, and his corporation provided both a company-funded pension and a 401(k) plan. Employees could contribute up to 15% of salary to the 401(k) plan to a limit that is now $10,500 per year. The company matched 50% of each employee's contribution.

As a result, George was nearing a retirement that would be funded with monthly pension benefits of $3,000 and Social Security payments of $1,000. In addition, he had saved about $500,000, but with no thought to structuring this sizable portfolio. Approximately $250,000 was in his employer's 401(k) plan in fixed-income securities, including money-market funds, long-term corporate bond funds, and long-term government bond funds. He had invested the other half of the $500,000 savings in **certificates of deposit (CDs)** with varying interest rates and maturity dates.

> **Certificates of deposit (CDs)** are savings certificates, generally issued by commercial banks, entitling the bearer to receive interest. A CD bears a maturity date and a specified interest rate, and can be issued in any denomination. The duration can be up to five years.

In many ways, George had exercised self-discipline and shown intelligence and foresight. He had saved a substantial sum in conservative investments that would not lose their value, but he had overlooked two key factors—inflation and taxes. The bulk of his portfolio was earning annual interest rates of 4% to 8%. Inflation from 1985 to 1990—the five years before he examined his investments—had averaged 4%, consuming a substantial portion of his investments' earnings. In addition, virtually all of his savings were tax-deferred. As a result, to pay those deferred taxes in retirement, he would have to withdraw more than $15,000 from his portfolio for every $10,000 that he wanted to spend.

Having functioned as a corporate manager and executive for more than 40 years, George viewed his retirement as his becoming CEO of George Lasaud Inc. His first action as CEO was to establish a goal for George Lasaud Inc.'s investment portfolio. This was to pay the CEO $50,000 to $60,000 per year in addition to his pension and Social Security, which would enable him and his wife to travel and be generous with their adult children. His second act as

CEO was to appoint us to serve as COO for George Lasaud Inc. to structure and manage his investments.

Enabling George Lasaud to reach his goal of generating $50,000 to $60,000 annually from his portfolio presented a challenge. We needed to restructure his investments so that (1) they would grow more rapidly and outpace inflation, and (2) he could minimize his tax burden.

To achieve the required growth, we had to increase investment risk. George could afford that risk because he had the base of $48,000 guaranteed annually by his pension and Social Security. During the three-year period from 1991 to 1994, we converted the fixed-income securities in his tax-deferred account into common stocks. We put 50% in **blue-chip,** dividend-paying common stocks, such as Ford Motor Company, Dow Chemical, IBM, General Electric, and GTE; 30% in mid-cap, **high-growth common stocks;** 5% in small-cap common stocks; and 15% in international **value stocks**—corporations based in the European Union and Japan. The tax-avoidance strategy was that, as the CDs matured, we bought investment-grade state and municipal **bonds** that incur no federal or state taxes.

Also defined in Chapter 1, **blue-chip stocks** are shares in large ($5 billion or more in market capitalization), long-established, successful corporations with a national reputation for high-quality products or services, and a dominant market share. As a stockholder (or shareholder), the investor owns a part of the company, so stocks are also called equity instruments.

Growth stocks are typically companies with high price/earnings (P/Es) reflecting the belief that the company will increase sales and profits over time faster than their competitors and the economy. The market should recognize that success and reward it with an increased share price. Recent examples include GE, Intel, Microsoft, Cisco Systems, and Home Depot.

Value stocks are those selected for their intrinsic value relating to the company's assets, cash flow, earning power, and dividend-paying ability. Value investors seek profit by trying to identify stocks that are temporarily undervalued in the belief that, at some point, the market will recognize that they are undervalued and will purchase the stock, driving the price up.

Bonds are IOUs or promissory notes from the federal government, state or municipal governments, or corporations. Bond issuers commit to pay bondholders a certain rate of interest over a certain period of time. The bondholder is a creditor of the issuing entity, not a part owner, like a stockholder. Therefore, bonds are debt instruments. Bonds are also called fixed-income securities because they guarantee how much income the holder will receive during the duration of the issue and when the principal will be repaid.

The strategy placed half of the money invested in common stocks in the safest, most conservative companies. Corporations like Ford and GE have vast resources, skilled management teams, dominant market share, and other tangible and intangible assets that provide assurance of their long-term viability. They also pay shareholder dividends. However, while you can be confident that they are not going to go out of business, their stock prices are not going to appreciate at a rate comparable to that of a small but successful, high-tech start-up company.

Therefore, we invested 5% of the money in such companies. Even in the unlikely worst-case scenario—failure by the start-up companies—George would have lost only 5% of his stock investments. On the other hand, if one of these small startups had proved to be the next Microsoft, Intel, or America Online, George would have become a multi-millionaire. In fact, neither the best-case nor worst-case scenario unfolded. The small-cap stocks provided better-than-average, although not spectacular, growth, and none went out of business.

We also allocated 30% of common-stock investments to mid-sized companies. These offer more stability and safety than the high-tech startups and more potential for growth than the blue chips. Because we live in a global economy, we invested 15% of the money in substantial, successful foreign stocks, such as Sony and Siemens. If the Japanese or European markets outperformed the U.S. markets for a period, these stocks would help compensate for setbacks among George's U.S. investments.

The result was that the portion of George's portfolio that was converted from fixed-income securities to common stocks grew from 1991 through 1994 at 12% per year, from approximately $250,000 to $335,000. From 1994 to 1999, the stock portfolio grew at more than 24% annually. This was two times the rate of growth during the first three years, when it was in transition from fixed-income securities to common stocks. While George knew that past performance would not necessarily guarantee future results, the portfolio that was valued at $500,000 in 1990 was worth approximately $1.4 million at the end of 1998, providing George and his wife with, in his words, "more money than I ever dreamed we'd have." Having hoped for a couple of weeks of European travel every year, the couple now rents a villa in southern France for two months every summer, inviting friends and flying the children in for visits. To sustain this unanticipated lifestyle, George withdraws less than 5% of his portfolio per year.

Lesson: Selecting the appropriate mix of investments—some for income, some for growth—and careful attention to the tax implications of those decisions can produce a nest egg that provides for all the CEO's hopes and dreams . . . and then some.

Harry Nicolopoulos, Inc.

The story of Harry Nicolopoulos illustrates the benefits of sound tax planning as a component of an overall investment plan. Harry had his retirement savings invested in standard bank CDs when he retained us as COO for his virtual company, and was paying the usual state and federal income tax on the interest. We were able to show him how to eliminate income tax ethically and legally.

Harry Nicolopoulos is a first-generation American with a strong ethnic heritage, an equally strong work ethic, and simple goals. In 1988, he retired at age 65 from a 47-year career as a manufacturing worker for a Fortune 500 corporation. He was to receive a $1,500 per month pension and about $1,000 per month in Social Security. He had paid off the mortgage on the small house where he and his wife had lived for their entire marriage and had saved $170,000 over half a century, investing it in CDs that were paying 6% to 7% annual interest.

A widower with no children, Harry said his goals were self-sufficiency and buying a new American luxury car every two years. As the newly appointed COO of Harry Nicolopoulos, Inc., we pointed out that, with prudent investment, he could reasonably provide considerably more luxuries for his retirement than his stated goal. He could travel, buy a beach home, begin an expensive hobby, or donate to charity. But Harry defined wealth with stark simplicity—require no charity, live in his own house, and buy a new Cadillac or Lincoln every two years.

Simple goals require simple investment strategies, and we reinvested his $170,000 in 10-year tax-deferred annuities that paid 9% per year. This reduced the annual tax burden on his investments from about $4,000 to virtually nothing, increasing his annual disposable income.

For five years, the CEO and COO of Harry Nicolopoulos, Inc. met annually, reviewed the virtual company's income statement and balance sheet, and made no changes. Every other year, Harry drove a new car to the meeting, and he was, according to his definition, wealthy. Then, in 1993, things got even better.

Like investment-grade bonds, long-term bond annuities increase in value as interest rates decline, since the annuities guarantee a fixed annual interest rate. In 1993, interest rates fell substantially below the 9% that Harry's annuities paid, so by converting the contract to a variable annuity, he was able to earn an effective interest rate of 13.7%. We then invested two-thirds of the money in a balanced portfolio of blue-chip, dividend-paying, corporate common stocks, and one-third in utility stocks and bonds. The objective was to build a portfolio that would offer at least moderate growth but would not decline sharply if stock prices dropped.

The result is that Harry now spends about $30,000 every other year from his portfolio, easily affording his new luxury car. Even with that spending, his $170,000 has increased to $600,000 in 10 years. He enjoys the life he dreamed of, with more money than he ever anticipated.

Lesson: Frugality and realistic goals pay high dividends.

June Washington, Inc.

A client referred June Washington to us in the spring of 1994. She was 63 years old, the widow of a man who had been a middle-manager with one corporation for 30 years. June had been a clerk in the local town government. Born during the Great Depression, which had bankrupted her father's business, June had a fear of common stocks and suffered from the misconception that bonds are safe and stocks are risky. As a result, she had insisted—over her stockbroker's recommendation—that 100% of her $775,000 portfolio be invested in highly rated municipal bonds, which were paying less than 6% annual interest.

A review of her Financial Physical (Appendix A) quickly revealed that her pension from the municipal workers' union and survivor's Social Security payments provided a sufficient income for day-to-day expenses. Therefore, she needed no fixed-income investments, even though they constituted 100% of her portfolio.

To make matters worse, she had purchased **callable** bonds and invested in funds comprising callable bonds.

When a bond is **callable,** the issuer (the governmental or corporate entity) can redeem it unilaterally from the investor at any point before its maturity. This could be disadvantageous when an investor's high-interest bond is called away in a lower-interest bond market.

Shortly after June became our client, the Federal Reserve Board raised interest rates, and consequently bond funds, including those in which she had invested, declined in value. In 1995, as the Fed lowered interest rates, a number of June's bonds were called. At that time, the stock market was rising, so, in seeking what she thought was the safety of bonds rather than the risk she perceived in stocks, she had invested with devastating inefficiency.

After convincing June to regard her investments as a virtual company and to assume the role of CEO, we as the COO reviewed the attributes, advantages, and drawbacks of the full range of debt and equity investment vehicles. We also listened carefully to June's description of what she sought from her investment portfolio.

June's three children were married and raising their own families in different regions of the country. She said that she would like to be able to add spacious guest quarters to her home that would offer comfort and privacy when her children and their families visited. In addition, she would like to be able to afford to visit them and her older brother and sister, who also lived a good distance from her.

Because she could live day-to-day in comfort on her pension and survivor's Social Security, we determined that she could afford to invest a portion of her $775,000 in the stock market, where it would appreciate and fund both the home renovation and the travel to visit her relatives. We sold 10% of her portfolio, which was invested in bond funds, in the spring of 1994 and reinvested it in large-cap, blue-chip stocks.

As her bonds either matured or were called, we reinvested the principal in blue-chip stocks as well. In this way, we gradually changed the balance of her portfolio from 100% bonds to two-thirds bonds and one-third stocks.

Over time, June saw the value of the stocks grow, and the dividends they paid increased as well. The dividends supplemented her pension and Social Security, allowing her to travel to visit her children and their families and her brother and sister. Had she so desired, she could have withdrawn money from her stock portfolio for additional income. The new balanced portfolio (two-thirds bonds, one-third stocks) was appreciating at almost 11% annually. However, June elected to withdraw nothing from her equities investments, so, in the first five years of this strategy, her total portfolio increased from $775,000 to nearly $1.3 million.

As a result, June has decided not only to add guest quarters to her home, but also to pay for the airfare when her children and their families visit her. Her children do not have to use their own vacation money to see her, and they have comfortable, private accommodations when they visit. This makes the family visits more frequent and more enjoyable for all. By her definition, June Washington is a very wealthy woman.

Lessons: Neither stocks nor bonds, nor any particular balance of the vast array of investment vehicles is right for all investors. Also, careful, expert analysis—not fear and other emotions—should govern asset allocation.

Lessons of Chapter 3

Saving is necessary, but not sufficient, to enjoy your ideal retirement—whether that involves part-time work, charitable contributions, or summers in France. You must also structure your investments, taking into account inflation, risk, cash flow, taxes, current age and life expectancy, and market trends. You must develop a custom-tailored business plan with your COO that fits your needs and the current market condition.

■ ■ ■

Professional's Toolkit

Debt Instruments Versus Equity Instruments

Most of your clients will know that they should consider both debt instruments, such as government or corporate bonds, and equity instruments, such as corporate common stocks, for their portfolios. Most will probably understand that, with a bond or other debt instrument, the investor loans a sum of money to an institution, receiving interest payments over the term of the loan and return of the principal at the end of the term. They will also probably understand that the purchase of corporate common stock constitutes ownership of a small part of a company.

The understanding of many investors—even intelligent, educated people who have amassed substantial six-figure portfolios—may not extend much beyond these rudimentary facts though. Furthermore, they may be confused by common misconceptions. One misconception that we encounter often is that bonds are safer than stocks. This misconception stems from considering only half the story, the relative yield of bonds and stocks but not their value.

An Investment Instrument's Yield

The yield of a bond is the interest the investor receives over the term of the loan to the bond issuer. The yield of a stock, if there is one, is the dividend paid to shareholders.

The yield of the bond is guaranteed at the time of purchase, so, if the bond issuer is a reliable entity such as the U.S. government or a large, profitable, highly rated corporation, that yield is, for all practical purposes, certain to be paid in full and on time. With common stock, the yield consists of quarterly dividends that the board of directors may vote to pay to shareholders. These dividends are not guaranteed when the investor buys the stock. The board votes to pay dividends based on the company's success and its need for cash. A company's history of paying dividends is not necessarily a reliable predictor of future dividends; if the company needs cash for expansion or other valid purposes, it may suspend dividends. Many companies pay no dividends, choosing to use the funds to finance product development or penetration of new markets.

When you consider the certainty of yield (bond-interest payments versus common-stock dividends), it is accurate to consider investment-grade bonds to be more reliable, more predictable, and, in this way, safer than stocks. But, as stated earlier, this is only half the picture.

An Investment Instrument's Value

The other half of the picture is the value of the investment. The value of shares of corporate common stock will, of course, fluctuate based on a variety of factors, including the growth and profits of the company, the market's view of the prospects of its industry, and the overall economic and investment climate. Over the long term, however, corporate common stock has been the most reliable investment in terms of capital appreciation. Even after major stock-market crashes, including those in 1929 and 1987, most stocks rebounded above their pre-crash highs. (See Figure 3.1.)

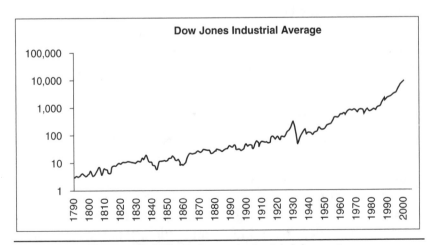

FIGURE 3.1 Dow Jones Industrial Average
Source: PaineWebber

While a bond's interest payments do not fluctuate, its value does. As interest rates and inflation rise, the value of a bond decreases. Why is this so? Let's say you buy a 15-year bond that pays 6% interest. Let's further hypothesize that three years into the 15-year term interest rates increase and new bond issues with the remaining term now pay 6.75% interest. You want to sell your bond to raise money for a summer beach home or a European vacation. Why would other investors buy your bond that pays 6% when they can buy a new issue that pays 6.75%? As the demand for your bond declines, so does its value.

Inflation can also erode the purchasing power of the yield, or coupon payment, of a bond. If an investor's 15-year bond pays 6% annually, but inflation increases by 4% per year, the investor is losing purchasing power.

Inflation results when a country's money supply grows faster than its economic activity, or, in other words, faster than the nation's output of goods and services. With more money available to purchase goods and services, people bid up the price of those goods and services, and prices increase. As a result, a given sum of money will purchase less and less over time and, in that way, becomes less valuable.

If the annual inflation rate is 12%, $1 will purchase only 88% as much on December 31 as it did on January 1. Economists usually express this thought by saying that the dollar is worth 88 cents, compared to its value at the beginning of the year. If, during that year, your investments grew by 12%, it looks to you as though you made a lot of money. Your $10,000 on January 1 has grown to $11,200. On paper, your investments grew, or appreciated, by $1,200, and indeed Uncle Sam will tax that $1,200 at the capital gains rate. But in reality—at the grocery store or car dealership—that $11,200 will buy what the $10,000 would have bought on January 1. So after paying the capital gains tax, you have less purchasing power from that investment than you did at the beginning of the year.

The misconception about bonds being safer than stocks also overlooks the callable nature of some bonds. We have seen many investors buy bonds without asking if they are callable or even knowing that this is a possibility. If a bond is called and the investor has his or her principal returned, what's the problem? Let's say a retired couple has paid off the mortgage on their home and counts on the 6.75% interest on $100,000 in bonds for the $6,750 they need to pay the annual property taxes. The bonds are called, returning the $100,000 in principal, but now bonds are paying only 6% interest. If the couple reinvests the principal in new issues, they will receive $6,000 per year and will have to use other income to make up the $750 difference.

All these comparisons are based on investment-grade bonds, such as highly rated bonds issued by the U.S. Treasury; fiscally sound and well-managed states or cities; or large, profitable, well-managed corporations. Many clients have come to us with high-yield bonds (sometimes called junk bonds) in their portfolios. These are low-rated bonds issued by low-quality companies that pay substantially higher interest rates than investment-grade bonds. These can be sensible investments for wealthy individuals who understand the risk and can afford to lose what they invest in junk bonds. But any of your clients who invest in high-yield bonds must understand that for the higher interest rate, they place at risk that total investment.

So, the common idea that bonds are safer than stocks, and therefore more appropriate for retired people, is as misguided and deceiving as it is simple. It does not even answer the right question, because the right question is not, "Which is safer—stocks or bonds?" The right question is, "Given this family's (this virtual company's) assets, income, needs, and dreams, what investment choices are the most sensible and effective for them?"

This is why you, as the COO of your client's virtual company, must ensure one of two conditions: Either you understand all the factors in asset allocation between debt instruments and equities, or you make available to your client the counsel of a qualified financial advisor who does.

Asset Allocation: What Kinds of Equity Instruments?

Once the CEO (your client), in consultation with his or her advisors, has determined the appropriate balance between debt and equity instruments, the COO must decide what kind of common stocks will make up the equity portion. As this book goes to press, growth stocks enjoy greater popularity than value stocks, reflecting a number of factors, including a strong **bull market** and an extended period of economic prosperity. However prudent investors know that no country's national economy expands forever and that, typically, three years of every ten will produce unfavorable market conditions. Therefore, one of the financial advisor's most important assignments is to recommend the proper balance of growth stocks, value stocks, and blue-chip stocks in the equities portion of the portfolio.

In a **bull market,** stock prices are increasing and optimism is the prevalent emotion. Bear markets, typically short-lived, are the opposite, defined as a decline in stock prices of 20% from the previous high. Market corrections, defined as a decline of 10%, now occur more frequently. The COO must educate clients about market volatility.

Asset allocation within the equities portion of a portfolio also demands consideration of U.S. versus international securities. In spite of America's global economic and technological leadership, more than half the world's equity value is located outside our borders. This means that substantial investment opportunities lie in foreign securities. Indeed, in any given year, a number of overseas markets outperform ours. The financial advisor must consider all the client's sources of income—salary, pension, Social Security, real-estate income, and all investments—and where those income sources are based. These factors, combined with global economic and financial conditions, will determine the appropriate balance of U.S. and international equity investments.

Tax Planning

Taxes are another key factor in determining the investment instruments you select for a client's portfolio. The COO of the client's virtual company must either be knowledgeable about the tax aspects of a client's investments or must recognize when the advice of a certified public accountant (CPA) or tax lawyer is required, and know where to obtain that advice. State and federal tax laws are so numerous and so complex, and change so frequently, that a virtual company may well need the expertise of a CPA or lawyer who specializes in this field. It is part of the COO's responsibility to help provide the information that the CEO needs, to raise the issues, and to ask the questions of the tax lawyer that will elicit the counsel the CEO needs.

Who practices tax minimization? Anyone who

- Buys a home rather than renting to deduct the interest portion of the mortgage payments.

- Buys municipal bonds whose interest payments incur no income tax.

- Invests in common stocks with the intention of retaining ownership to pay long-term capital gains taxes on the appreciation, rather than paying ordinary income tax on, for example, a bond's interest payments.

- Invests in tax-efficient mutual funds or with a tax-efficient money manager.

- Invests in a tax-deferred annuity to pay taxes in retirement when a reduced income will place him or her in a lower income-tax bracket.

Tax minimization is certainly not the only factor in investment planning and is usually not even the most important. But in most cases, it deserves consideration.

International Stock Investment Vehicles

In discussing portfolio diversification, we advocate inclusion of international stocks as a hedge against a downturn in the U.S. economy vis-à-vis Western Europe, Japan, and other developed regions. The most common international stock investment vehicles include American Depository Receipts (ADRs), foreign ordinary shares, closed-end country funds, and open-end mutual funds. There are also investments that are constructed to mimic the performance of certain foreign market indices. These investments combine features of closed-end and open-end funds, but actively trade on major U.S. exchanges.

- **ADRs** are certificates issued by U.S. banks. Each certificate represents a fixed number of shares of the underlying foreign companies. American Depository Receipts trade on U.S. stock exchanges in U.S. dollars, and their prices are available in the newspaper. They settle and clear just like any other U.S. stock. In order for foreign companies to qualify for ADR listings, their financial information must conform to U.S. accounting standards, which differs from foreign ordinaries. Listed ADRs benefit from the liquidity that an exchange listing offers. Because ADR prices tend to track the underlying shares that trade in their local markets, they can be affected by currency fluctuations.

- **Foreign ordinary shares** trade in the local market in which the company is located. Therefore, purchasing ordinary shares directly from a local exchange would entail converting U.S. dollars into that country's currency. Before doing this, investors should also consider that each country has its own accounting standards, reporting requirements, and custody and settlement procedures. Some investment firms offer investors the ability to purchase foreign ordinary shares in U.S. dollars. Offering this capability also means that any dividends would be paid to the investor in U.S. dollars, instead of in the local currency.

- **Closed-end country funds** are professionally managed and invest in a variety of securities from a particular country or region, thus offering diversification across a defined market. They are issued like stocks, but have a limited number of shares determined in the initial public offering. Most country funds are listed on the New York Stock Exchange or the NASDAQ and their prices are quoted in newspapers. Country funds offer liquidity through the exchange market, and, depending on investor demand, they may trade higher (at a premium) or lower (at a discount) than the fund's net asset value. The net asset value is the market value of the securities and other assets held by the fund, net of liabilities.

- **Open-end mutual funds** are also professionally managed and invest in a variety of securities. International funds comprise only foreign securities while global funds may also include U.S. securities in their portfolios. Investors choosing an international or global fund may select from those of various investment objectives, such as growth or value. Mutual funds are priced once a day, and sales are made at net asset value, which may be higher or lower than the price an investor originally paid.

Goals, Balance, and the Long-Term View

"Money is always there but the pockets change;
it is not in the same pockets after a change,
and that is all there is to say about money."

—Gertrude Stein

Understanding Asset Allocation

The first decision for the newly appointed CEO and COO is this: How should the virtual company invest its assets? In other words, what asset allocation will the COO recommend? This chapter includes information that is a bit more technical than that in the preceding chapters—but still understandable, we hope—as we focus on the key concept of asset allocation. The fundamentals we explain here are brought into play in many of the remaining chapters.

Asset allocation is the selection of diverse, uncorrelated types (or classes) of investments to maximize portfolio return and minimize risk. The word "uncorrelated" is key. It means that the various types of investments that are selected will perform differently in any given set of economic and market conditions. The types of investments will complement each other; when one is up, the other will be down, smoothing out the performance of the overall portfolio and reducing its volatility.

Two assets that pay 12% annually and maintain identical per-share prices in times of stable inflation and interest rates are said to be perfectly correlated, and are assigned a correlation coefficient of 1. These assets' prices would rise and fall together, so the investor owning both would have no portfolio diversification. Your COO's task is to recommend a combination of investments that is less than perfectly correlated, or even negatively correlated, to achieve your goals with a comfortable risk level.

Modern Portfolio Theory

To maximize return and minimize risk, asset allocation follows the principles of Modern Portfolio Theory (MPT), which was developed in the 1950s by an economist and educator named Harry Markowitz. His thinking revolutionized asset allocation and earned him a share of the 1990 Nobel Prize for Economics. Before MPT, investment analysts—amateur and professional—selected portfolio assets by attempting to predict the ups and downs of the prices of individual stocks and other vehicles.

Some individual investors—even serious, knowledgeable ones—still try to predict the short-term movement of individual stocks by avidly, almost obsessively, following televised or Web-based commentary and advice by supposed experts. Professional financial planners abandoned this approach decades ago, and we strongly recommend that individual investors follow suit.

Since MPT advocates seeking a balance among various types of assets based on their risk and return, it is not just putting your eggs in different baskets. It also involves making sure that those baskets complement one another. An important part of MPT is the concept called the Efficient Frontier. This refers to composing your portfolio in a way that provides maximum return for a given degree of risk, or alternatively the least amount of risk for a given return.

Equities Diversification

Within equities, diversification can be according to sector, for example selecting stocks in pharmaceuticals, electronics, machine tools, financial services, aerospace, software, and automotive manufacturing. Diversification can entail balancing growth stocks against value stocks and buying shares in small-cap, mid-cap, and large-cap corporations.

You may balance U.S. Treasury bonds against small-cap growth stocks. The bonds will provide a fixed income with virtually no risk of default, but they also offer little hedge against inflation. The stocks pay no fixed income or dividends, and entail substantially more risk than U.S. Treasurys because the companies may go out of business, but they offer the potential for growth that far outpaces inflation.

Over the long term, globally diversified portfolios usually offer greater return at less risk than do well-diversified, but 100% domestic, portfolios. Because the economies of different countries and different regions of the world are involved, there is less correlation among domestic and foreign securities than among domestic securities, even when they are chosen from different business sectors. National factors such as monetary and fiscal policy, political stability, economic growth, and demographics affect each country's securities.

How important is an intelligently diversified asset allocation? In *Determinants of Portfolio Performance II: An Update,* Gary Brinson, Brian Singer, and Gilbert Beebower assert that 93% to 95% of a portfolio's results—maximum return, minimum risk—can be attributed to asset allocation. They attribute only 5% to 10% of performance to market timing, specific securities selected, and the portfolio manager's style. The analysis and the advice of many large national and international financial and investment firms are consistent with this view.

Stocks, Bonds, Mutual Funds, Cattle Futures?

What types of investment instruments should your financial planner recommend? Again, that depends on your individual circumstances and goals. A retired couple, each receiving Social Security and large pensions from stable organizations, may have all the fixed income they require and might invest 100% of their savings in common stocks. Another couple with no pension may invest a substantial portion of their portfolio in U.S. Treasurys and investment-grade corporate bonds to provide a fixed income.

As we have stated previously, one popular misconception holds that bonds are safer than stocks. A false conclusion often drawn from this false notion is that retired people, with limited capacity to earn money, should always buy bonds and never buy stocks. However, on an annualized basis, from 1924 through 1996, stocks returned 12.7% versus 5.4% for intermediate-term government bonds (Treasury bills) and 3.8% for cash. During that same period, annual

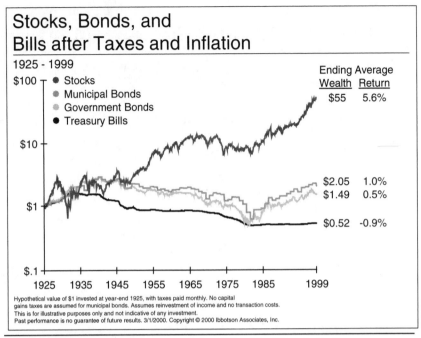

Stocks, Bonds, and Bills after Taxes and Inflation

1925 - 1999

Ending Average
Wealth Return

$100

- ● Stocks
- ● Municipal Bonds
- ● Government Bonds
- ● Treasury Bills

$55   5.6%

$10

$2.05   1.0%
$1.49   0.5%

$1

$0.52   -0.9%

$.1

1925 1935 1945 1955 1965 1975 1985   1999

Hypothetical value of $1 invested at year-end 1925, with taxes paid monthly. No capital
gains taxes are assumed for municipal bonds. Assumes reinvestment of income and no transaction costs.
This is for illustrative purposes only and not indicative of any investment.
Past performance is no guarantee of future results. 3/1/2000. Copyright © 2000 Ibbotson Associates, Inc.

FIGURE 4.1 Accumulated Wealth After Inflation

inflation averaged 3.5%. From 1968 through 1998, stocks returned 12.62%, bonds 8.77%, and cash 6.71%. Inflation was 5.21%. Figure 4.1 shows accumulated wealth after taxes and inflation of stocks, bonds, and bills from 1925–1999 on $1 originally invested.

Historical performance offers no guarantees and is often not a reliable predictor of the short term (less than 10 years). Nonetheless, more and more investment professionals are concluding that the safest investment vehicle for the long term is corporate common stock, intelligently diversified according to the MPT and Efficient Frontier principles. Professor Jeremy Siegel of the Wharton School at the University of Pennsylvania says, for example, that common stocks' superior return on investment (ROI) makes them safer than bonds.

Harry Dent, author of the 1999 book *The Roaring 2000s: Investor Strategies for the Life You Want* and other books, has tracked the number of 49-year-olds in the economy and superimposed the value of the stocks in the S&P 500 index over that graph, adjusting for inflation. He concludes that the potential impact of the baby boomers on the stock market makes U.S. common stocks an attractive investment in the coming years.

"The secret to successful investing is understanding very fundamental long-term trends, and buying when companies and investments in those sectors are undervalued, when no one wants them," Dent says in *The Roaring 2000s.* "Large company stocks and international equities will outperform in the coming decade as they did in the Roaring '20s. Bonds and small-cap stocks will underperform."

Is Dent correct in these specific sector predictions? Nobody knows. That is the argument for diversification. Your financial advisor's objective should not be to beat the market, but to craft a long-term investment strategy that will move your virtual company toward your individual life, investment, retirement, and bequesting goals. It is tempting to chase short-term gains, especially when the media and the Internet present case study after case study of supposedly successful day traders. Of course, it's possible to make a lucky gamble. But stock picking for the short term will always be just that—a gamble.

It comes down to this: One of the greatest business and financial geniuses of all time, J.P. Morgan, was wrong. Asked for a formula for successful investing, he said, "Buy low, sell high." It would be a great idea, but for one factor: No one can do it. It is not how Morgan became one of the wealthiest men in the world. He achieved wealth the old-fashioned way, by building highly successful and profitable businesses.

After Asset Allocation—Hold to the Plan

Once you and your financial advisor have devised an asset allocation that makes sense, the most important principle of successful investing is to hold to the plan.

Does this mean you never adjust asset allocation or ownership of specific securities? Of course not. One of the COO's chief duties is to free you of constantly checking your investments by monitoring business, economic, and financial trends and constantly evaluating their impact on your portfolio. We strongly agree with Harry Dent's statement in *The Roaring 2000s,* "Life should be interesting; investment and financial planning should be boring. You should focus on what you enjoy and do best in life and let an objective financial advisor put you on the proven system for building the wealth that you deserve to achieve your life goals."

You should meet with your financial advisor annually, semi-annually, or more often if market conditions dictate, to review your portfolio's performance and to see if significant changes in your personal situation or in the market call for asset reallocation.

The Wealth Story of Phillip and Carol Vitale, Inc. illustrates the important investment principle of asset allocation.

□ □ □

Phillip and Carol Vitale, Inc.

In 1993, Phillip and Carol Vitale, both about 40 years old, approached us to become their financial advisors. Phil was driving two successful careers in parallel. He was facilities engineer for a substantial manufacturing corporation in southern California, where he supervised 15 people, and was responsible for heating, cooling, plumbing, lighting, and so forth for a factory and the associated offices—the entire physical plant from parking lot to roof.

Although these responsibilities would consume the energy and workplace productivity of most capable engineers, Phil successfully founded an independent consulting firm in his spare time. With his employer's knowledge and authorization, he established Long Beach Consulting Engineers. The firm made his facilities-engineering expertise available to owners and managers of small commercial, healthcare, and educational facilities who needed help with the maintenance of their buildings, but could not cost-justify hiring someone with Phil's experience full time. At first, Long Beach Consulting had a total employment of two—Phil and his wife, Carol. She did the bookkeeping and answered the phone while he was at his day job at the plant. Over the years, he built up the consulting practice, eventually establishing offices and hiring an engineering and clerical staff.

Phil and Carol had three children in elementary school. They had accumulated about $100,000 by saving in bank CDs of one-, three-, and five-year terms, starting in the early 1980s. At that time, this type of CD paid 12% to 13% interest, but during the 1980s, those rates gradually declined to 7% to 8%. The interest was taxed as ordinary income, just like Phil's salary, so the Vitales were paying almost 40% of it in federal and state taxes. With inflation eroding the purchasing power of the CDs each year, the savings looked great on paper, but, in fact, the Vitales were not accumulating the resources they knew they would need for three college educations and their own comfort and security.

By the early 1990s, money-market funds were paying about the same interest as the CDs, and Phil and Carol had transferred their savings to this type of account as the CDs matured. This had the advantage of high liquidity, affording the Vitales the ability to reallocate the investment with minimum administrative hassle and no penalty fees.

When the Vitales founded Phillip and Carol Vitale, Inc. in 1993 and appointed us COO, Phil was adamant about investing the $100,000 differently. He wanted to own stocks—and only international stocks at that. He had read that most of the safest large companies to invest in were based outside the United States, and to compound Phil's desire to invest outside the United States, family lore had it that Carol's uncle had lost all his money in U.S. stocks.

While this was certainly not the typical plan we would recommend, we listened to Phil's wishes and agreed to an international stock portfolio, as long as the companies the Vitales invested in were large enough to have global earnings ability. This meant that the companies were large multinational firms whose revenues were not dependent on a sole country. We also made Phil promise to allow us to add a U.S. component to the portfolio within the next several years, with the ultimate goal of paring the international portion to 30% of the total portfolio.

Before we were hired as the COO, the investment had been growing at 7% to 8% annually. With the reallocation, it grew at an average annual rate exceeding 16.5% for four years, from $100,000 to just over $185,000. Had the Vitales left the $100,000 in the CDs, it would have accrued to less than $135,000. Furthermore, the growth of the stocks was taxed as a long-term capital gain—28% then and 20% as this book goes to press—versus the approximately 40% tax rate on the interest earned by the CDs.

Financial advisors who take a cookie-cutter approach to investment counsel might say the decision to place the entire $100,000 in international stocks was too risky, counting injudiciously on a bull stock market. Such an advisor would say we should have invested a substantial portion in bonds and U.S. securities. However, we developed the investment plan by taking a comprehensive view of the

Vitale's finances, goals, and specific investment requests. Phil's corporate salary and consulting-firm income, both of which were dependent on the U.S. ecomony, provided a fixed income that was more than sufficient for day-to-day expenses, both necessities and luxuries. The Vitales were long-term investors, counting on the portfolio for retirement in two to three decades and for their children's college educations, the earliest of which was 10 years away. This made a total reliance on the stocks of established, prosperous corporations a sound, albeit not traditional, investment strategy.

At about the time that the original $100,000 had appreciated to $185,000, Carol inherited $80,000 from her mother, and Phil sold shares of his consulting firm to two partners, netting him $35,000 after taxes. This totaled $300,000. With these growing resources, the CEOs of Phillip and Carol Vitale, Inc. asked us if early retirement was a realistic goal. They were in their mid-40s and asked, Can we invest the $300,000 so that Phil can work full time for 10 years and help his partners build the consulting firm and then retire at approximately age 55? He wanted to leave the manufacturing firm at that time and cut back his involvement in the consulting firm to one or two days per week, with summers off. And they still wanted to educate the three children along the way.

We calculated that they would need a $1 million portfolio at age 55 to realize that dream. Combined with Phil's expected pension and, later in life, his Social Security, they could draw off $50,000 from the portfolio (5% of the $1 million) and maintain both their standard of living and their savings.

Relying on MPT, we recommended two actions. (1) Allow us to diversify the portfolio so that two-thirds is U.S. based and one-third is international, and (2) save and invest $10,000 per year for the 10 years. Phil and Carol agreed. The couple also planned to pay capital gains taxes and income taxes on dividends and interest from earned income, assuming that Phil's salary and income from his business would continue to grow.

In early 1997, we divided the $300,000 equally among three private asset managers—the international blue-chip program in which they were already invested; a U.S. blue-chip value portfolio; and a U.S. mid-cap growth portfolio. At that point, Phil began the annual $10,000 additions to his portfolio. By mid-1998, the original $300,000, the two annual $10,000 deposits, and the appreciation totaled $450,000. With the autumn market correction that year, it dropped to $360,000. But by the end of 1998, it had rebounded to $450,000, and by year-end 1999 the portfolio was worth more than $600,000.

These stock price fluctuations contain an important lesson. It was crucial that Phillip and Carol Vitale, Inc. not divest their portfolio when the value declined in the third quarter of 1998. Had they done that, they would have sacrificed the tremendous gains they made in the fourth quarter of 1998—one of the strongest quarters in recent stock market history.

Remember, the key is time in the market, not timing the market. History reports that most ten-year periods comprise seven good years and three poor ones, but no one knows when the strong and weak years are coming. Sticking with your investment plan will work to your benefit. For long-term planners, weak years bring bargain prices and, therefore, increased savings and investing. If you panic and sell, you may lose your savings.

The result is that the Vitales are three years into this plan and have earned an annual return of 26.5%. With this fast start, they need only 7.38% per annum for the next seven years to achieve their ten-year goals. The diversification using MPT has worked.

A snapshot of the Vitale's plan in 1999 shows that despite their U.S. value portfolio having earned less than 5% that year, their international portfolio earned more than 50% and their mid-cap portfolio earned about 30%.

At the end of the first quarter of 2000, however, this snapshot looks different. The Vitales' international portfolio is down more than 5%, the value portfolio is up almost 10%, and the U.S. mid-cap portfolio is up almost 20%. The design is working. Risk management is in place, and we keep Phil focused on the importance of that, despite his continual nagging desire to be in the number-one program for growth that particular year. He now realizes it doesn't work that way. Hindsight is always 20/20. Prudent investing using MPT should allow participation in the hot sector each year, whatever that happens to be. Next year something else will probably be in favor and an MPT approach makes it more likely that you'll have a small portion invested there already.

So the Vitales are adhering to the plan and will try to increase annual savings. Saving at the prescribed level, they are encouraged and focused. They look forward to college for their kids and retirement in their mid-50s. They have wealth by their definition.

Lessons of Chapter 4

Diversify your portfolio with complementary securities, guided by the principles underlying Modern Portfolio Theory. Create and adhere to an investment plan.

Resist the temptation to outguess the market, irrespective of your neighbor's or brother-in-law's boasting. He's very lucky or, more likely, lying.

Review the portfolio at least annually and make adjustments according to your financial advisor's analysis of long-term interest rates, inflation, and other business and economic factors, as well as changes in your personal situation.

■ ■ ■

Professional's Toolkit

Allocating Your Clients' Assets

Asset allocation, as described in this chapter, is step 2 in the following four-step, comprehensive investment planning and execution process.

1. **Goal Setting.** This involves a thorough Financial Physical, as we call it, using the information requested in Appendix A. This enables you and your client to review total wealth; liquidity demands; timetables; capacity to tolerate short-term, market-driven fluctuations in returns; and tax liabilities and avoidance.

   In *Alice in Wonderland,* the heroine encounters a fork in the road and asks the Cheshire Cat whether she should travel to the right or the left. The Cheshire Cat asks where Alice is headed, and she replies, "Anywhere will do." The sage feline's counsel is, "Then either road will take you there." The same applies to investing. No financial advisor can help a client reach a goal that the client has not defined.

2. **Customized Asset Allocation.** Applying the concepts of MPT and the Efficient Frontier allows you to balance the expected market returns and market risks of various classes of investment to achieve the results that will best meet your client's individual situation and goals.

3. **Customized Investment Recommendations.** Within the selected investment classes, it is your responsibility to recommend to clients individual instruments, considering taxable, tax-free, and tax-deferred alternatives; ROI rates; and other factors.

4. **Ongoing Portfolio Review.** Every 6 to 12 months you and your client should review portfolio performance together to ensure that the investments selected are in tune with economic and market trends and conditions, and your client's goals. Additionally, you should review the due diligence assessment of each management firm within the client's portfolio to ensure that the manager is adhering to the investment style you have chosen and that no material changes have occurred in terms of staff or focus.

After you agree on asset allocation, one of your most important duties as COO of your client's virtual company will be to urge the CEO not to jump in and out of investments according to the latest comment on television or in an Internet chat room. Why? Because no one can anticipate or outguess the market.

Should your clients decide to gamble on their own, however, you cannot afford to participate. Asset allocation is governed not only by the client's goals and the sound diversification principles of MPT, but also by the laws of the Unified Prudent Investor Act (UPIA). In *The Journal of Financial Planning,* Eugene Maloney, an investment-firm lawyer, wrote, "These [UPIA] statutes impose significant new duties on professional trustees, which, if inadequately performed, could result in liability to the trustee regardless of the positive returns of trust portfolios."

The Different Types of Risk

Risk minimization is one of the two stated goals of asset allocation (the other being return maximization). Investors incur several kinds of risk, including the following:

- **Market risk** is the financial uncertainty of the future market value of a portfolio of assets. As the stock, bond, and other markets fluctuate, so too will the instruments within them.

- **Credit risk** is usually associated with bonds, and means simply that the issuer may be unable to make interest payments or repay the principal. With U.S. government securities and bonds of blue-chip corporations, this is not a practical factor. However, no one can afford to ignore the credit risk associated with certain municipal and corporate issues.

■ **Liquidity risk** tends to compound other risks and can be most damaging for institutions that are experiencing financial difficulties, creating a need for immediate cash.

Specific liquidity risk means that a particular institution may lose liquidity, especially if its credit rating falls or something else halts or inhibits trading.

Systematic liquidity risk affects all participants when an entire market loses liquidity. Financial markets tend to lose liquidity during periods of crisis or high volatility.

■ **Interest rate risk** means that when interest rates increase, the prices of bonds typically decrease, and vice-versa.

■ **Inflation risk** means that the increasing cost of living can quietly erode an investment's returns. Secure investments, such as U.S. Treasury bills and CDs, incur substantial exposure to this kind of risk. They usually have lower returns and yields that, over time, may not outpace or even keep pace with inflation and taxes.

■ **Currency risk** is the gain or loss on international stock or bond investments vis-à-vis the U.S. dollar. If an investor holds a Japanese mutual fund, and the yen is weak relative to the U.S. dollar, the fund will have lower returns.

CHAPTER 5

Pitfall 3:
Respond to
Tipsters and Telemarketers

"Bulls make money and bears make
money, but hogs just get slaughtered."
—*American proverb*

The Temptation to Stray From a Successful Plan

It's one thing to have an effective investment strategy, individualized to your risk tolerance, personality, lifestyle goals, and financial circumstances. It can be another thing to stick to the plan—
even when it is performing successfully.

To many readers, that opening statement may sound strange, or
even incredible. After all, why would you be tempted to stray from
a strategy and plan that was achieving your own goals?

Investors violate, or completely abandon, strategies that are
achieving their objectives often and for many reasons. One reason is
the thrill of the hunt—the sense of competition and adventure in
seeking out the next Microsoft, Wal-Mart, or amazon.com—fueled
by an overabundance of investment information on the Internet.
Some investors entertain, and even indulge, the idea that they can
beat the pros, relying on their ingenuity, cleverness, and nose for a
bargain. In the motion picture *Working Girl,* Melanie Griffith's character, a secretary, outsmarts investment bankers and corporate exec-
utives by piecing together apparently unrelated facts from newspaper and magazine articles, including a gossip column. She not only

gets rich, but also wins the heart of the prince, Harrison Ford, and vanquishes the wicked stepmother—or, in this case, the treacherous mentor, Sigourney Weaver. In Hollywood, where Peter Pan can fly and never grow old, this can happen—but not in the real world, or at least not often.

Another reason that investors abandon success is the timeless allure of supposed get-rich-quick schemes. Unfortunately, these siren calls to false riches often drown out a little voice in the back of the investor's head saying, "If this sounds too fast, too easy, and too certain to be true, it probably is." That voice is almost always right.

A third temptation that lures investors from effective plans is envy—the false impression that everyone else is making a fortune in the stock market. This silly notion can result from taking a neighbor's bragging or television coverage of day trading at face value.

In still other cases, investors wander from success because of something as simple as a clever telephone pitch from a salesman they do not know and, more importantly, who does not know them.

The following four Wealth Stories illustrate these temptations and the havoc they can cause, along with solutions—some full and some only partial.

□ □ □

Jack Infante, Inc.

Jack Infante built a successful practice as a highly skilled stonemason over 30 years in Rhode Island. He and his small crew could build something as simple as a flagstone walk from the driveway to the front door, or as difficult as a seawall to restrain Narragansett Bay in a storm. His wife, Maria, supplemented their lifestyle as a hairdresser and did the books for the masonry business. By 1990, at age 54, Jack had saved approximately $340,000 and paid off the mortgage on their home. The Infantes had accumulated little debt—a small home equity loan for a daughter's wedding, two car loans, and a boat loan. All were manageable within their income.

At the recommendation of the CPA who handled their business and personal taxes, the Infantes came to meet with one of us. The Infantes had often mentioned to their CPA that they wanted to retire in eight to ten years, and he knew they were saving for that retirement.

He knew enough to ask if they had a comprehensive financial plan, which they did not, and he also knew that such planning was not his specialty. The CPA warned me that Jack was entranced with the stock market and was always touting a stock that someone had told him about or that he had discovered on the Internet.

Jack talked an excellent game about the winners he'd picked and the money he'd made. He was not trying to fool anyone; what he said was the truth as he saw it. But, from preparing the family tax returns—including capital gains and losses—the accountant knew this was not the full story. Jack was not alone in having a better memory for his winners than his losers.

At our first meeting, Jack made it plain that he trusted his own ability to analyze and select stocks. He said he was a wide reader and active Web surfer. Forewarned, I had come to the meeting equipped with a stack of articles from home fix-it and do-it-yourself (DIY) magazines on building stone walls, walkways, fireplaces, and other projects. I also brought handouts from DIYer sessions at a local home center on building your own backyard brick barbecue.

"I've read all these articles, and I read every issue of *Family Handyman* and *Bob Vila's American Home,*" I told Jack. "In addition, I participate in an Internet chat group on home DIYer projects and, every summer, my wife and I do a home-improvement project together. So, I guess I know as much about stone masonry as you do, even though it's been your profession for 30 years, and even though you do more projects in a month than I've done in my entire life."

Jack did not become indignant even for a minute. He was bright enough to understand the point. He asked if I meant that he could have no input into the types of investments that would make up his own portfolio.

"Not at all," I replied. I then drew an analogy to Jack's masonry business. "If a customer tells you she wants a garden wall, you discuss her needs and how she envisions the project. You present alternatives with advantages, disadvantages, and cost estimates. You recommend one approach, correct? Then, you and the customer agree on the wall design, prepare a plan, and turn it over to your team of professional masons to build. Once the masons start construction, however, the customer does not tell them exactly how to place each stone."

Jack agreed. That was exactly how he worked with customers.

"We will take a similar approach with your investment portfolio," I told him. "You and Maria will tell me how you want to live your final working years and your retirement. I will present investment alternatives and recommendations. Once we agree on a plan, I will turn over the individual buy and sell decisions to professional money managers. Together, you, Maria, and I will review their performance and your goals every six months against the **S&P 500** and other benchmarks. We will make adjustments as appropriate, including, if warranted, changing money managers."

> The Standard & Poor's Index (**S&P 500**) is a measurement of the fluctuating value of 500 widely held stocks. It is one of several indices commonly used to evaluate the performance of money managers, mutual funds, and individual portfolios.

Jack liked the approach and formed Jack Infante, Inc., visualizing his investment portfolio as a business. He viewed himself as the CEO, and I became the COO.

At the first planning meeting of Jack Infante, Inc., which was attended by Jack, Maria, and me, I listed every stock the virtual company owned. For every single security, I asked the boss such questions as the following:

- Why did you buy it and why do you still own it?

- What analyst or investment firm provides research on it?

- Does the broker who recommended the stock keep in touch with you, even if it has declined in value?

- How do you evaluate the performance of the advice you receive from each broker or information source?

Jack realized that he could not answer most of those questions, and, again, he did not need the point explained. He knew which stocks he'd bought, and, in most cases, which had appreciated and which had declined in value. But he did not know the average rate of return of his portfolio, and he had not kept track—in rigorous, mathematical terms—of whose advice had paid off in the long run and whose had not. He realized that he had not been running his virtual business with anything like the analysis, planning, and everyday common sense that had made his masonry business a success.

As this book goes to press, I have been overseeing the business plan of Jack Infante, Inc. for 10 years. Jack and Maria have both retired. For fixed income, they rely on Social Security and income from the masonry business, which their two sons have taken over and are purchasing from their dad over time. Their investments are 100% corporate common stocks—50% large-cap, 25% mid-cap, and 25% international. If the Infantes did not have the base of fixed income, this asset allocation would probably be too uncertain from a cash-flow standpoint. In other words, without other fixed-income sources, they might have to sell stock to use the money for everyday needs at a time when the price was low or when a sale was disadvantageous for tax purposes.

The portfolio that was worth $340,000 10 years ago is now valued at more than $1 million, even though the Infantes make periodic withdrawals. They have replaced their sailboat with a larger model and travel to parts of the United States they have always wanted to visit. By their definition, they have achieved wealth.

Jack retains his interest in stocks and his exhilaration at the thrill of the hunt. But, with Maria's support, I have persuaded him to make a hobby of small purchases of stock—never more than 100 shares of a relatively inexpensive growth stock. Jack makes these purchases as cash flow permits, without invading the assets of the Infantes' virtual business. When he makes a little money, they go on a three-day weekend to an inn in Vermont; when he loses, they cut back on luxuries for a few weeks. Happily, Jack does not jeopardize the couples' financial wellbeing, and, as he often observes, "It's less expensive than belonging to a country club."

Lesson: If you want a stone wall that will outlive you, hire a good mason and let him do his work. If you want an investment portfolio that will outlast your retirement, take the same approach with a qualified financial planner.

Francis Charleton, Inc.

Frank Charleton forged a successful career as a corporate executive and, with his wife Abigail, was a reasonably self-disciplined saver, encouraged by a generous 401(k) plan at work. By 1989, Frank, then 52 years old, and Abigail, 49, had accumulated $175,000 but had not invested it appropriately in view of their personal circumstances. Frank was working full time, earning a salary on which the couple could live comfortably. So, they did not need income from their investments, but they wanted to retire in 10 to 15 years, and they were passing up the potential appreciation of corporate common stock.

When they approached us as their financial advisors that year, the Charletons were vague and even contradictory about their goals and plans. Early in the initial discussion, they mentioned early retirement, before age 60, for Frank as a goal. Later in the same discussion, they referred to Frank's retirement at 65. They had not even settled on a destination, let alone a road map to get there. They had given no thought to how much income they would need from their portfolio to supplement his pension and Social Security, or how much Abigail would need if, as the odds indicated, she outlived Frank, and therefore his pension and Social Security. As a result, they had no conception of how large an investment portfolio they needed, let alone whether they could save that much by 1997, when Frank would reach age 60, or by 2002, when he would be 65.

They seemed to think that a happy, secure retirement would happen on its own. It won't.

Another inconsistency materialized in that first discussion. Both Frank and Abigail sought growth from their investments and were aggressive risk-takers, entirely comfortable with the risk that a growth strategy would entail. Yet, their investments were low-growth and ultra-safe.

As we combed through the Charletons' investment statements, we observed a problem. Interbrokerage transfers, liquidations of mutual funds and tax-deferred annuities, and other investment turmoil revealed that the Charletons sought and accepted advice from many sources, but told none of them the full story. To them, every stockbroker or financial advisor they met was smarter than the last—until they met the next one. They jumped from this mutual fund to that annuity with no overall plan, just the urging of a salesman seeking an immediate commission. With a get-rich-quick mentality, the Charletons were actually enriching a series of salesmen and saddling themselves with an underperforming investment portfolio.

We helped them determine that they would need an annual retirement income of $80,000 by the year 2002 to maintain their working-years lifestyle. We then showed them how to arrange it:

Payment Source	Income per month	Income per year
Social Security (estimate at age 65)	$1,200	$14,400
Pension (approximate)	$2,300	$27,600
Withdrawal from investment portfolio	$3,179	$38,150
Totals	$6,679	$80,148

In order to make a 5% annual withdrawal to equal the $3,179 per month required by this formula, the Charletons would have to build their $175,000 portfolio of 1989 to $763,000 by retirement. If they did that by 1999, Frank could retire at 62. To accomplish this, we recommended a portfolio of growth-oriented mutual funds. We further specified, and the Charletons agreed to, no withdrawals for 10 years and regular contributions of $2,000 per month, preferably more. Had the Charletons adhered to the plan, publication of this book would have found them, with the bull market of the intervening decade, securely and happily retired.

However, the desire for a shortcut to riches and the seductive pitches of franchise salesmen distracted the Charletons from their sensible plan. They became partners in two multilevel marketing businesses, one in environmental products for the home and the other in cosmetics and herbal medicines. Both failed. Their errors were classics: They underestimated the investment of time and money these enterprises would require and had trouble focusing on the bottom line because of the many partners involved. The Charletons entered both ventures with no relevant experience and paid dearly for their poor judgment.

In 1995, a downsizing at Frank's company eliminated his job. He was unemployed for six months, finally accepting position at a substantially lower salary. The toll was not just financial, but also emotional, burdening him and Abigail with constant worry about their elder years. At the same time, their franchises began to founder, causing them to raid their retirement savings to keep the businesses afloat and meet ordinary living expenses. Since they were not yet 59½ years old, the withdrawals from tax-deferred savings incurred penalties in addition to income tax. This ravaged their savings, compounding the worry and emotional strain.

We repeatedly urged them to stop deceiving themselves with get-rich-quick fantasies, jettison the unprofitable ventures, moderate their lifestyle, and return to the financial plan we had all agreed on. For nine years, the Charletons ignored these entreaties. Finally, in 1998, they cut their franchising losses. By that time, Frank had earned a promotion and raise that returned him to close to his peak salary, and they reinstituted their financial plan. However, they had missed nearly a decade of one of history's strongest bull markets. Their portfolio is actually smaller than it was in 1989. Had they simply left their original $175,000 untouched, and had it grown at 12% annually, which many portfolios did during this period, they would now have $577,567, an appreciation of more than 300%. If they had added just $1,000 per month, they would now have more than $800,000.

Adhering to their own plan would have provided a secure, comfortable retirement, instead of their current situation—work and worry.

Lesson: Get-rich-quick schemes generally enrich those who sell them to suckers seeking effortless wealth. Consistent adherence to a sensible financial plan with a competent advisor is not easy, but it does work.

Angelo and Gina Orsini, Inc.

In 1990, at ages 50 and 47, Angelo and Gina Orsini decided to formulate their savings into a virtual company with a plan for their retirement years. They had saved $225,000 and had invested it predominantly in large-cap stocks, mid-cap stocks, and corporate bonds.

With input from us as their financial advisors, the Orsinis determined that financially and emotionally they could endure more risk, and therefore potentially increase the growth rate of their investments. We recommended, and they agreed to, an asset reallocation to 100% equities—60% blue-chip value stocks and 40% blue-chip growth stocks. Although the Orsinis made periodic withdrawals during the 1990 to 1995 period, their portfolio continued to grow. By 1995, it was worth approximately $350,000. The plan was working.

In early 1996, Gina joined an **investment club**. Investment clubs can be highly beneficial, encouraging saving and helping members learn to evaluate investments analytically and dispassionately. But, in this case, the investment club led to a vague dissatisfaction by Gina that the Orsinis' investments were not growing fast enough, but with no definition of that term. She and Angelo discussed her misgivings and, without consulting us, they opened an account with a stockbroker at another firm and began trading **options**.

Investment clubs are chartered by the National Association of Investment Clubs and comprise individual investors who save, analyze investment vehicles, and invest in them regularly and communally. See www.naic.com.

An **option** is part of a class of securities called derivatives, which means these securities derive their value from the worth of an underlying investment. It gives the buyer the right, but not the obligation, to buy or sell an asset at a set price on or before a given date. Investors, not companies, issue options.

Buyers of *call options* bet that a stock will be worth more than the price set by the option (the strike price), plus the price they pay for the option itself.

Buyers of *put options* bet that the stock's price will drop below the price set by the option.

Options are a highly speculative investment vehicle. Experts who understand their nature and risks can use them successfully, but neither the Orsinis nor their broker had the required knowledge or experience. The Orsinis had no appreciation for the risk they were incurring.

The Orsinis sold options under a covered-call strategy involving 5,000 shares of stock that they owned in the company Gina had worked for. The stock had a total value of $75,000. Gina had accumulated these shares by 30 years of participation in an employee stock option plan (ESOP). Under their covered-call strategy, if the stock increased in price, the purchaser of the options would have the right to buy the Orsinis' shares for the price at which they were selling when he bought the options. This dangerous tactic worked for a short time. The stock did not increase in price, so the purchaser of the options did not exercise them. The Orsinis retained the stock and received a premium on the sale of the options.

Then profits at the company rose, driving up the stock price. The holder of the options exercised them, calling away the Orsinis' stock. This drained their portfolio and caused them to incur capital gains taxes. Since they had owned the stock for years, they were selling it for more than they paid for it. To replace those investments, the Orsinis purchased calls on other companies' stock that they thought were going to increase in price. They were wrong, so they lost on those options too.

If all this sounds complicated, it is. Options are extremely complex instruments. No investor should consider them unless he or she understands them thoroughly or works with a financial professional who does. The Orsinis were not knowledgeable, nor was the broker who opened their account and executed their trades.

After one year of these misadventures, the Orsinis closed the options account and returned to the financial plan they had agreed on earlier. By late 1999, their portfolio had grown to more than $600,000. They enjoy peace of mind, help their children finance their grandchildren's college educations, and support favored charities.

The options fiasco was a brief anomaly, and the Orsinis enjoy wealth by their definition.

Lesson: Avoid investment instruments you do not understand, especially those involving high risk.

Dr. Steven Kuchinski, Inc.

Steven Kuchinski is an unmarried, highly successful surgeon who earns an excellent salary and saves plenty of money to secure his retirement. But Steven can become so enchanted with what he views as get-rich-quick opportunities that he takes silly risks and almost invariably loses. What's worse, he does it again and again.

In 1991, at age 45, Steven was making a six-figure salary and had saved approximately $300,000, which he had invested in CDs, money-market mutual funds, and corporate common stock. He owned a $900,000 home with a $250,000 mortgage. On the recommendation of his mentor at work, he engaged us as financial planners saying that he wanted to devise a savings and investment plan that would enable him to retire by age 62. He also said that because of his relatively young age and high salary, he was willing to incur a high degree of risk to reach this goal. We agreed that for those reasons Steven was indeed in a position where more-than-usual risk made sense. What we failed to realize at that first meeting, however, was that we had a vastly different idea of what constituted sensible risk than Steven did. To us, sensible risk meant a portfolio of common stock in successful companies. As it turned out, to Steven sensible risk meant a series of fly-by-night schemes and scams where his favorite grifter-du-jour promised instant wealth.

In early 1991, we invested half of the $300,000 in American blue-chip value stocks and the other half in blue-chip growth stocks. For a retired couple dependent on their investments for current income, such a portfolio allocation would have been too aggressive. But for Steven, we judged it to be appropriate.

In that year, the growth portion of the portfolio increased 60% and the value portion increased 40%, for a total portfolio of $450,000 at year end. Steven was satisfied, but just barely. When we warned that it was unrealistic to count on these growth rates year after year, Steven seemed not to believe us; in fact, he seemed not to be listening. During the next two years, 1992 and 1993, the growth slowed dramatically. The portion of his portfolio comprising so-called growth stocks was actually stagnant for the two years, while the blue-chip portion increased 14% in 1992 and 20% in 1993.

Near the turn of the year from 1993 to 1994, Steven's impatience and his susceptibility to get-rich-quick temptation got the better of him. Against our advice, Steven withdrew $230,000 to invest in a start-up company that made exotic test instruments for which, as it turned out, there was no market. He not only lost $230,000, but he also failed to learn a lesson from it. He was then back where he had started three years earlier.

Steven Kuchinski's Portfolio 1991—1993

	On January 1	On December 31
	1991	
U.S. value stocks	$150,000	$210,000
U.S. growth stocks	$150,000	$240,000
Totals	$300,000	$450,000
	1992	
U.S. value stocks	$210,000	$240,000
U.S. growth stocks	$240,000	$240,000
Totals	$450,000	$480,000
	1993	
U.S. value stocks	$240,000	$290,000
U.S. growth stocks	$240,000	$240,000
Withdrawals for get-rich-quick schemes	—	($230,000)*
Totals	$480,000	$300,000

This decision by Steven Kuchinski, over our strenuous objections, flushed the tremendous gains of three years down the drain.

At the outset of 1994, Steven directed us to shift the entire U.S. growth portion of his portfolio to international stocks, which had been registering substantial appreciation. At this time, he had $150,000 in U.S. value stocks and $150,000 in international stocks. Both the domestic and international markets remained even throughout 1994, and this was reflected in Steven's portfolio, which had the same value at year end as it had on January 1. Once again, Steven's attempt to outguess the market failed. The best we can say is that this time it did not cost him much.

In 1995, the U.S. portion of Steven's portfolio increased 45% and the international portion, into which he had shifted a substantial share of his assets, grew 13%, providing a total value of $386,000 at year end. Steven kept jumping around. At the beginning of 1996, he insisted on selling his entire international portfolio and reinvesting the money in U.S. value stocks. Once again, we reminded Steven that no one can outguess the market, and that the best approach is to devise a strategy and execute it consistently over time. But we were never successful in convincing Steven to take this approach.

In 1996, Steven's U.S. portfolio grew almost 20%, but nonetheless he was seduced by a Caribbean real estate development scheme in early 1997. Once again, against our counsel, Steven withdrew more than $100,000 for a shaky condominium/resort development project. For one year, he received promises and rosy predictions. By the end of the year, it was obvious that the project was foundering, and Steven's investment was gone.

Steven Kuchinski's Portfolio 1994—1997

	On January 1	On December 31
1994		
U.S. value stocks	$150,000	$150,000
International stocks	$150,000	$150,000
Totals	$300,000	$300,000
1995		
U.S. value stocks	$150,000	$217,000
International stocks	$150,000	$169,000
Totals	$300,000	$386,000
1996		
U.S. value stocks	$386,000	$459,000
Totals	$386,000	$459,000
1997		
U.S. value stocks	$459,000	$460,000
Withdrawals for get-rich-quick schemes	($110,000)	—
Totals	$349,000	$460,000

As this chart reveals, Steven virtually erased a gain of more than $100,000 with another of his get-rich-quick schemes, which always turned out to be scams.

Over the next two years, until late 1999, Steven left his investments in U.S. blue-chip value stocks. At the end of 1999, he once again insisted that we shift 100% of this U.S. value portfolio to a U.S. growth portfolio. He continually tried to outguess the market and consistently failed. At the dawn of the year 2000, Steven has a portfolio of $530,000. Had he stuck to the plan we agreed on in 1991, his portfolio would have totaled approximately $1.7 million. That difference, nearly $1.2 million dollars, is the price of two get-rich-quick, quixotic adventures and constant asset reallocation, stemming not from a professional's market analysis, but from an amateur's effort to outguess the market.

Steven has resolved that, starting in the year 2000, he will leave his investments alone for seven to ten years. We are skeptical, but hopeful.

Steven Kuchinski's Portfolio 1998—1999

	On January 1	On December 31
1998		
U.S. value stocks	$460,000	$506,000
Totals	$460,000	$506,000
1999		
U.S. value stocks	$506,000	—
U.S. growth stocks	—	$530,000*
Totals	$506,000	$530,000

Against our advice, Steven Kuchinski shifted his investments from value stocks to growth stocks, because the latter had been outperforming the former for more than one year. Unfortunately, Steven made the transfer too late in the year.

If Steven Kuchinski had not disturbed our asset allocation, his investments of $300,000 in 1991 would have appreciated to approximately $1.7 million by the end of 1999, between 3 and 3.5 times the $530,000 portfolio that his get-rich-quick schemes and attempts to outguess the market left him with.

Lesson: The race to retirement security is won by the turtle— slow, steady, sensible—not the jackrabbit. It took Steven nine years to learn this lesson; it's better to learn it from the outset.

Lessons of Chapter 5

Get-rich-quick schemes usually make the originator rich (and sometimes incarcerated) and the investor poor. Avoid them.

No one is smart enough to outguess the market. Don't try.

Avoid derivatives. These are investment instruments with no inherent value, but a marketplace value governed by the price of other vehicles. Stock options, described in the Wealth Story of Angelo and Gina Orsini, Inc., are one example. Commodities and interest-rate futures contracts are another. Derivatives are volatile and extremely complex. Leave them to the super-wealthy and super-sophisticated investors who can make money on them sometimes, and to the suckers, who, when they experiment with derivatives, almost always lose.

Invest sensibly, according to a plan, with top-flight professional assistance, and stay with the plan.

■ ■ ■

Professional's Toolkit

Helping Clients Further Understand Asset Allocation

Throughout this chapter, we use the term "asset allocation," the selection of investment vehicles for an investor's portfolio. But the apparent simplicity of the asset allocation, or structure, of a portfolio can be deceiving. As a financial service professional, you owe it to your clients to look below the surface and ensure that they understand their own asset allocation.

In *The Wall Street Journal* of November 23, 1999, Jonathan Clements provided several excellent examples of this principle. He sketched a hypothetical $300,000 retirement portfolio consisting of $150,000 in bonds in a taxable account and $150,000 in the 401(k) plan of the investor's employer. Clements pointed out that, on the surface, this looks like a 50%–50% asset allocation between stocks and bonds. However, the investor will owe approximately one-third of the money in the 401(k) account in deferred taxes, so the effective value of that portion of the portfolio is only $100,000.

As a result, the actual asset allocation is not 50%–50%, but 60%–40% favoring bonds.

Tax liabilities can distort the view of a portfolio in many ways. Two portfolios of the same nominal worth will be significantly different if one contains tax-deferred instruments and the other comprises taxable assets.

Clements made another pertinent point in this article. He said that people often count the equity in their homes as a retirement asset. But, if they sell the home, they will have to use a sizable portion of the cash for their next home. "At best," Clements said, "you may be able to tap a part of your home's equity, by trading down to a smaller place or taking out a reverse mortgage."

Financial advisors must be knowledgeable about these sorts of factors or bring someone who is well-informed to the discussion table with their clients.

CHAPTER 6

Pitfall 4:
The Cookie-Cutter Approach—
How *Not* to Handle Asset Allocation

"Money is round. It rolls away."

—Sholem Aleichem

Looking at the Total Financial Picture

Cookie-cutter asset allocation is the lazy financial advisor's way to design a client's portfolio with minimum effort and no thought. It's an approach in which the financial advisor considers a few characteristics of an investor without having a full, rich, subtle understanding of the investor's goals, assets, and personality, and has a knee-jerk response to those limited facts.

For example, one popular cookie-cutter approach to asset allocation for retired folks is, "You're not earning a salary, so you need maximum safety and fixed income. You should own investment-grade bonds, issued by the U.S. Treasury, other federal agencies, and blue-chip corporations—period." No other factors are considered.

Many retired couples enjoy fixed incomes from pensions, Social Security, and other sources that reduce or eliminate their need for fixed income. In addition, many retirees these days are relatively young and in good health. They may be looking forward to 25 years or more of retirement. In these cases, they need protection against inflation much more than they need fixed income, and the best anti-inflation insurance is provided by a common stock portfolio structured according to the principles of Modern Portfolio Theory, or MPT, which was discussed in depth in Chapter 4.

For reasons such as these, the quick, thoughtless, knee-jerk approach to asset allocation is almost always ineffective. This is true even when the cookie-cutter approach is dressed up in apparently sophisticated computer software. Some financial advisors plug a client's statistics into portfolio-design software, applying no human intelligence, judgment, or understanding of the client as a person. They then recommend whatever the computer printout says, representing it as scientific asset allocation. It is still a cookie-cutter approach to what should be a thoughtful, strategic exercise.

□ □ □

Laura Wheelwright, Inc.

Laura and Malcolm Wheelwright had been married for just over 40 years when he died in 1993, leaving her with sufficient funds to support herself, but with no experience in managing money, no investment plan, no spending plan, and no trusted advisor to lean on. Married just after college, Laura was only 62.

Malcolm had forged a long and successful sales career at one of the nation's largest food processors. The Wheelwrights lived in New England, which constituted Malcolm's sales territory for the bulk of his career. On more than one occasion, Malcolm was offered promotions involving larger or additional territories, but he always declined. New England is small enough and densely populated enough that he could travel to the large wholesalers who were his customers and usually return home the same night. At most, he would be gone for one or two nights. Being able to limit his time away from home was more important to him and Laura than the salary increases and the extensive business travel that larger territories would have brought.

The Wheelwrights had three children who were the center of their lives. Family suppers, plus Malcolm's being available to attend evening teacher conferences, help the children with homework, and simply be present in the home, were of paramount importance to the couple. Laura forsook career ambitions to stay at home to raise the children, so they were making sizable financial sacrifices for the family-oriented lifestyle they valued. Nonetheless, the Wheelwrights were able to fulfill their dream of sending all three children to college, where diligence and effort earned all three excellent grades and launched them on successful careers.

As the kids advanced through high school and left for college, relieving Laura of many of her duties as homemaker and mother, she volunteered for church and civic charities and causes. She chauffeured elderly folks from their church to medical appointments and on shopping excursions. Meanwhile, Malcolm not only earned all the family's money, but he also managed it, although not as skillfully as he gave himself credit for. As a result, when he died the finances were not in especially good shape, and Laura was totally unprepared to manage them.

Like many married couples, one spouse had assumed the total responsibility for financial management, and the other spouse had been all too ready to cede the responsibility and the labor involved. This is dangerous because if the spouse who does not handle the finances survives the one who does, he or she is unequipped to be financially self-sufficient.

The Wheelwrights were not unusual in this respect. Fifty-nine percent of respondents to a readership survey published in the October 1989 issue of *McCall's* rated themselves as either "somewhat competent" or "not competent at all" in money management. According to the September 1995 issue of *Working Woman*, 54% of the women surveyed for a national study reported "fear of making a mistake" as a reason for procrastinating with financial decisions.

The problem with the Wheelwrights' finances was not one of volume, but focus. They had not come to view their investments as a virtual company and had not found a financial advisor to design and execute a savings and investment plan that would enable them to achieve their life goals.

The combination of Malcolm's earning power and Laura's household frugality left her, at his death, with a home with no mortgage, a pension and Social Security that totaled approximately $3,200 per month, zero debt, and investable assets of $350,000. Of the $350,000, approximately $250,000 was in IRA rollover accounts. The balance of $100,000 included the proceeds from a life insurance policy and checking and savings accounts.

The Wheelwrights had been traditional, conservative investors purchasing CDs; money-market funds; government and corporate bond funds; and blue-chip securities, diversified in telecommunications, automotive, and pharmaceuticals.

Shortly after Malcolm's death, Laura met with three stockbrokers, each of whom Malcolm had entrusted with a portion of the Wheelwrights' investments. This illustrates Malcolm's scattergun approach to investing. He and Laura would have been better off if he had identified one trusted advisor and worked with that person on an intelligent allocation of all their assets. From each of the three brokers, Laura sought advice on how to invest the IRA rollover accounts and the common stocks scattered in the three accounts. The receptions that she received at the three firms were virtually identical and totally unsatisfactory. None asked her about investments that were held by the other two firms or deposited in other accounts. All were condescending and left Laura with the impression that they thought she was naïve and indecisive. As she later said, "They seemed as though they couldn't be bothered with me."

Laura did not realize that Malcolm had inadvertently preconditioned the brokers not to take Laura seriously. In a misguided effort to protect her, he had told them that if he died first, she would need them to invest for fixed income because, as he put it, "Laura loves to shop." In fact, Laura was quite sensible in her shopping. Her enthusiasm for it and for the bargains she invariably found at discount stores led Malcolm to the mistaken belief that she was spending money extravagantly. So following Malcolm's guidance, the brokers dismissed most of what Laura said and urged her to invest the majority of the assets in bond funds to generate a fixed monthly income.

Laura demurred that she was receiving more than $3,200 per month in pension and Social Security. She said that this fixed income was sufficient to meet her day-to-day needs. For the reasons already discussed, the brokers seemed not to pay attention to her and at the end of the process, Laura found herself with a portfolio of fixed-income investments.

Because all three brokers had given her the same advice, Laura suppressed her doubts and told herself, "They must know more about this than I do." In fact, Laura's own instincts were closer to an intelligent investing strategy than what the three professionals had told her. She should have been taking advantage of the upward surge of the stock market during the 1990s to build her investments. Instead, she watched as rising interest rates in 1994 drove down the share value of her bond funds. She noticed that the value of her bond funds was declining, but the brokers characterized these as paper losses and told her not to worry. The bond funds were still paying monthly income, they told her, and that income was being reinvested.

For the next few years, Laura watched her funds lose ground while her friends celebrated their investment gains made in equities. She made periodic withdrawals from her portfolio to accompany them on vacations, but was troubled by their tales of growing investment portfolios while hers dropped from $350,000 to $265,000.

Finally, in 1998, Laura confided to her closest friend that she did not understand how her investments were declining as rapidly as they were. Her withdrawals, she said, did not add up to the $85,000 difference between $350,000 and $265,000. Her friend understood her alarm and strongly recommended that she meet with us, as we had been her financial advisors for several years.

"You're only 67," the friend told Laura. "You could easily live another 20 years and, at this rate, you'll be broke long before you die."

Laura took the advice and established Laura Wheelwright, Inc. At our first meeting, she said, with considerable exasperation, "What happened to my money?"

A thorough review of her statements and records revealed factors she had overlooked. For example, when she withdrew funds from her portfolio, she failed to take into account her federal and state income tax obligations on IRA distributions. She did not realize that when she withdrew $5,000 to splurge on a vacation, she depleted her portfolio by $7,000, including federal and state income tax withholdings.

The next problem we confronted was the nature of the underlying investments in Laura's mutual funds. She owned not only government and corporate bond funds but also Real Estate Investment Trusts (REITS), which had underperformed although they had still produced income.

We recommended an asset allocation in several types of mutual funds including **balanced,** global, growth, equity, income, and

S&P index funds, structured for conservative growth along the lines described in the section on MPT in Chapter 4. The strategy was to leave these funds untouched until she reached age 70½ and to live on the pension and Social Security. She would then begin to take at least the IRS-required minimum distributions from the IRAs. This required Laura to stop the withdrawals that were permitting her to accompany her friends on their vacations. While she regretted this, she understood the rationale and realized that self-restraint would be necessary for several years to ensure that she did not outlive her savings.

> **Balanced funds** seek to protect capital by diversifying among bonds, corporate common stock, and corporate preferred stock.

"I was frugal when Malcolm was alive and we were saving for the kids' educations, so I can be frugal again," she said. In the first year of Laura's new financial regimen, her three children, for whom she and Malcolm had worked so hard, pooled some of their own vacation money to give her a Caribbean cruise on which her two best friends were booked.

As this book goes to press, it has been less than two years since the restructuring of Laura's portfolio, but already she has seen the account balance appreciate. For the first time since Malcolm's death, she is not worried about outliving her funds. Furthermore, she is confident that when she starts her minimum distributions, her portfolio should continue to grow and provide a rising income stream.

Lessons: A married couple should make sure that both spouses are familiar with family financial matters. That way, either spouse would have the knowledge, capability, and comfort level to continue the prudent management of the estate, in the case that he or she outlives the other spouse.

It is most beneficial to work with one trust financial advisor, rather than follow the piecemeal advice of multiple advisors, each of whom handles a portion of your investments.

Don't be embarrassed to ask questions of your financial advisor, and to reiterate your goals periodically.

Fred and Susan Baxter, Inc.

Fred and Susan Baxter had been working with a broker whom they felt relied more on his software and his own investing bias than on his clients' wishes.

Fred retired as a product and marketing manager at a household-name corporation in 1990 at age 62. He and Susan had saved and invested to accumulate $1 million. They had paid off the mortgage on their waterfront house on Massachusetts' North Shore between Boston and the New Hampshire border, valued at the time at $800,000. In addition, they received a fixed income of $115,000 per year from Fred's pension and Social Security, and Susan's part-time job as a court stenographer. She found the work fascinating and had no desire to quit, even though she was just one year younger than Fred.

When Fred retired, the Baxters' broker plugged their ages, job status, and investable assets into an asset-allocation computer program which called for only 30% in equities and 70% in cash and fixed income. The Baxters said this made no sense; they could easily live on their existing fixed income of $115,000 annually. In fact, they were saving nearly $30,000 per year.

The Baxters did not need fixed income to live on and wanted to invest for growth, so they could increase their international travel, yet leave a substantial bequest to their children. They also said that their health was good and that they expected a long retirement. Unaided by their broker, they realized that, over time, inflation and the inevitably rising cost of living would reduce the purchasing power of their fixed income.

For all these sound reasons, the Baxters wanted to assume moderate risk to give their portfolio the opportunity to appreciate. The Baxters were sufficiently intelligent and sophisticated to present their broker with the factors that should have governed asset allocation. But the broker did not listen to them; he simply studied his computer printouts and allowed himself to be governed by his own overly cautious nature.

Still, the Baxters did not give up. Every time one of their Treasury bills matured and they asked their broker for an equities recommendation, he would reply, "The market is shaky" or would give some other weak excuse for staying out of the stock market. His refusal to listen to them drove the Baxters to seek a professional financial planner. Their neighbor, a long-time client of ours, referred them to us. Thus began Fred and Susan Baxter, Inc.

When the Baxters arrived at our office, the retired couple came armed with a notebook generated by a computer and provided by their broker. The notebook had cost them $1,000 and was one inch thick. It looked impressive on the surface—full of small type, pie charts, and graphs. But it was virtually impenetrable even to us as professional financial planners, let alone someone not professionally educated in investments. The plan left the Baxters completely and understandably puzzled. When we finally figured it out, we realized that the strategy, for all its formulas and equations, made no sense in light of the Baxters' circumstances and goals.

The Financial Physical that we reviewed together at that first meeting revealed that both Fred's and Susan's parents had lived well into their 90s and that this was typical of their aunts and uncles as well. It was immediately evident to us that the Baxters had a sensible, well-founded reason for seeking a growth portfolio. They sought a hedge against inflation and the assurance that they would not have to sell their seaside home to finance their later years.

As a result, we reallocated their assets into a mix of 60% common stocks and 40% U.S. Treasurys. The equities portion was broadly diversified to minimize the ups and downs of the market, encompassing 50% growth stocks and 50% value stocks.

The strategy was intelligent, and market trends proved to be on the Baxters' side as well. The portfolio reallocation was made in early 1994 and by year-end 1995, the equities portion of their holdings had increased by approximately 40%. Interest rates increased steadily during 1994, driving down the prices of their remaining bonds. In addition, our firm was forecasting better-than-average growth in the equities markets for the coming five years. As a result, by late 1998, only 10% of the portfolio remained in U.S. Treasurys.

The Baxters understood the strategy and had confidence in it. They recognized that they did not need immediate income. From his career, Fred was familiar with the demographic analysis of Harry Dent, which was mentioned briefly in Chapter 4. The Baxters echoed Dent's outlook that the prospects were strong for an upward surge in the stock market—perhaps to levels unmatched in the past or future. Even during the early years of our relationship managing Fred and Susan Baxter, Inc., the couple realized that they would be able to leave a substantial inheritance to their children. As a result, they decided to prepay their inheritance taxes with an irrevocable insurance trust. (A more complete discussion of this and other estate planning strategies and tools occupies Chapters 10 to 15.) The Baxters purchased what is called second-to-die life insurance through the trust. When they both die and their estate passes to their children, the insurance policy proceeds will help pay federal and state estate taxes.

When the Baxters formed their virtual company in 1993, their estate totaled $1.8 million, including real estate. By late 1999, it was worth $4.5 million. As a result, we informed the Baxters that it was time to revisit their estate plan, and we facilitated a meeting with their estate lawyer. The Baxters added sophisticated estate planning instruments, including a Qualified Personal Residence Trust (QPRT, described in Chapter 15) and a Charitable Remainder Trust (CRT, described in Chapter 14). These and other strategies (described in Chapter 10) should be seriously considered—with the advice of an experienced estate lawyer—when your assets grow significantly above $2 million.

Unlike the Wheelwrights, the Baxters set up their investments like a virtual company and hired a financial advisor while both spouses were alive. Both husband and wife have been intimately involved in the formulation and execution of the plan. Regardless of who dies first, the surviving spouse will be thoroughly prepared to continue in financial peace and security.

Before forming Fred and Susan Baxter, Inc., the CEOs had identified an accountant to handle their taxes and a lawyer to handle their estate documents, but both professionals were operating independently of one another. As the COO of Fred and Susan Baxter, Inc., we convened the team so we could work together in the Baxters' best interest.

In the early years of our relationship, the value portion of the Baxters' equities portfolio performed most strongly, but later the growth portion outpaced it. Early on, Fred would constantly ask, "Why don't we put all our money in whichever sector is the strongest at the moment?" Having observed the fluctuations for several years, he now knows why: You never know in advance what direction any given investment sector will take.

The Baxters stick to their investment plan which is no longer one inch thick but is now totally understandable, adjusting according to our firm's forecasts for the economy, trade, inflation, and other macroeconomic factors. They are in the enviable position of having difficulty spending all their disposable income. Aged 72 and 71, Fred and Susan must now, by law, withdraw money annually from their IRAs, which frustrates and angers them.

"We don't need the money and we don't want it," they say.

As a result, we as the COO of their virtual company effectively order them to spend money. The kids are self-sufficient and don't want or need their parents' money. The Baxters' favorite charities are taken care of in their estate plan.

"Travel. Fly first class. Pick the top luxury resorts," we urge. "At this point, even with thorough estate planning, approximately half of every dollar you do not spend will go to Uncle Sam when you die. So you might as well enjoy it now."

Frugal by nature, the Baxters indulge in such spending habits only with encouragement but they are learning. And with their family histories, they may have a decade or two left to spend the money they have so carefully accumulated.

Lessons of Chapter 6

Working with a financial planner who considers just a few characteristics about you and then applies a generic, off-the-shelf asset-allocation plan will probably not produce the results you want. As the COO of your virtual company, your financial advisor must take the time to learn your individual circumstances and design a financial and investment plan to suit you.

■ ■ ■

Professional's Toolkit

Asset Allocation and Diversification

People often confuse the terms "asset allocation" and "diversification," using them interchangeably. Asset allocation is the process of investing in different types of investments, such as stocks, bonds, and cash. Diversification refers to purchasing different instruments within those types. For example, within common stocks, you might buy shares in 30 different corporations. In other words, asset allocation and diversification are successive steps in structuring a portfolio to achieve an investor's goals.

The investor's goals provide a starting point in discussions with clients. Retirement, paying for children's college education, and buying a home are three typical goals of saving and investing. Many of your clients will have all three of these goals at different, and perhaps overlapping, times in their lives. These and other goals will likely appear and disappear—intensify and fade—as time passes and circumstances change. The investment strategies you develop for clients must adjust to these changes.

The appropriate investment strategies for retirement, college, and home could be called, respectively, growth, income, and capital preservation. With the client's goal(s) in mind, you need to determine the level of risk he or she can sustain both financially and, usually more importantly, emotionally. In other words, how much risk can the client endure in order to maximize the return on the investments? Ask your client such questions as the following:

- If your assets decline in value in the short run, will you be concerned about your long-term security?

- Do you feel a strong urge to check your portfolio more often than every couple of weeks?

- How important are long-term goals (such as retirement in 20 years for clients in their early 40s) versus short-term goals (such as buying a home within five years)?

- Given good health, do you have confidence in your earning capacity during the coming 10 years?

Financial advisors should consider asset allocation and diversification only after the client's goals are defined, his or her capacity for risk is determined, and the optimum risk/reward ratio is calculated. Macro asset allocation is our term for the decision-making process of dividing a client's funds among various types of instruments, as stated previously, such as stocks, bonds, and cash. Micro asset allocation is our term for the subdivision of, for example, stocks into growth and value; large-, mid-, and small-capitalization; U.S., European Union, Far East/Pacific; and advanced economies versus emerging markets.

Intelligent asset allocation does not necessarily require macro allocation into more than one type. For instance, a couple nearing retirement who will receive a reliable fixed income from pensions and Social Security that is sufficient to sustain their standard of living, may have a macro asset allocation of 100% common stocks. On the micro level of asset allocation, this couple would almost certainly divide those stocks among several of the subcategories of stocks listed in the previous paragraph. It is a safe generalization to say that most of our clients have a macro asset allocation that encompasses more than just one type of investment at some, if not all, points in their lives.

Asset allocation is a crucial step in investment planning, accounting for more than 90% of a portfolio's total ROI, according to Ibbotson Associates.

Diversification, which was also defined at the outset, refers to spreading investments among a number of instruments within each asset class, or type. For example, within U.S. blue-chip common stocks, you might choose companies in several sectors— auto/transportation, such as Ford and Cummins Engine; pharmaceuticals, such as Pfizer and Bayer; chemicals, such as Dow and DuPont, and so forth. Along with most investment analysts, we believe that once you diversify among 30 instruments within a class, further diversification provides little or no marginal value. Depending on how much money your client has to invest and on your knowledge and professional relationships, you can diversify your clients' portfolios by selecting individual stocks, different money managers, or mutual funds.

One regrettable and dangerous result of the strong bull markets of the late 1990s is that many people—particularly those who are not financial professionals but who manage their own investments—have been abandoning asset allocation and diversification to pour everything into U.S. technology growth stocks. One wag put it this way, "Nowadays, people think that diversification means owning Oracle in addition to Cisco Systems."

A 100% concentration in U.S. technology stocks would have served investors well throughout 1998 and 1999. Will it continue? History says not. How long will it last? No one knows. Informed, planned, goal-oriented asset allocation and diversification remain essential to long-term investment success. Without this discipline, your clients are not investing. They are gambling.

CHAPTER

7

Pitfall 5:
Spread Your Investments
Among Many Brokerages and Banks—
Give No One the Whole Picture

"I am always looking for people who can do a better job than I can."
—*T. Boone Pickens*

"The surest way for an executive to kill himself is to refuse to
learn how and when and to whom to delegate."
—*J. C. Penney*

The Need for One Comprehensive Plan

Some people can't see the forest for the trees, but the investors described in this chapter have the opposite sight problem. They can't see the trees as anything more than individual trees, or in this case, singular investments.

The discussion of Modern Portfolio Theory (MPT) in Chapter 4 and the illustrations of its principles throughout the book illustrate how intelligent, planned diversification can minimize risk and maximize efficiency, or return, of a portfolio. But problems arise when investors seek diversification for its own sake—not as part of a comprehensive financial plan—and omit the COO of their virtual company.

If you were going to build a house, and you called a roofing contractor requesting a design, a bid, and then the actual roof, the contractor would ask for two things: the plans for the house and the name of the general contractor—the COO of the construction project. Suppose you told him, "There is no general contractor and no plan, and I'm not going to tell you anything about the house. Here's $20,000. Design and build me a roof, and deliver it intact to a certain address in 90 days."

If you were dealing with a sensible, reputable roofer, he would laugh and walk away. At best, he would tell you that he had to know what the house was like overall before he could build a roof. He would not take your money.

As silly as this example sounds, it is exactly how many people approach their investment portfolio. What's worse, many supposed financial professionals accept these assignments. A prospective client walks in with any amount of money—$10,000, $100,000, or $1 million—and says, "Please invest this so it will grow."

Too often, the financial advisor or broker is so glad to have a new client that he or she does not ask, "Are these your total investable assets? If not, what sorts of investments and other assets do you have?" The client may not volunteer this information out of ignorance or embarrassment, and the financial professional may not inquire for fear of offending a new client. Both are wrong. The investor is not exercising intelligent stewardship of his often hard-won assets, and the financial professional is not providing the counsel that the client deserves.

The investor needs the same two things that the prospective homebuilder needs—a plan and a COO. With substantial portfolios, the COO will diversify among various types of investment instruments. But he or she will be doing so following a comprehensive plan that reflects your total financial picture and goals.

□ □ □

Roger and Hazel Fonseca, Inc.

Roger and Hazel Fonseca are diligent savers who avoided Pitfall 1 (Don't Save During Prime Earning Years), but fell deeply into Pitfall 2 (Save Blindly Without Goals or a Plan), and Pitfall 5 (Spread Your Investments among Many Brokerages and Banks, Giving No One the Whole Picture). When they first approached us as their financial advisors, they had brokerage accounts with four different firms with holdings of stocks, municipal and corporate bonds—both **zero-coupon** and **coupon**—and a host of mutual funds. The mutual fund types included growth stocks, blue-chip stocks, and bonds. The Fonsecas even had a safety deposit box full of U.S. savings bonds. Roger's 401(k) account was invested predominantly in corporate stock and bond funds.

A **zero-coupon** bond is a bond sold at a deep discount from its face value and pays that full face value at maturity. It does not pay periodic interest payments to an investor; instead, an investor receives his or her return on investment upon the bond's maturity. The return is equal to the difference between the bond's price at purchase and its face value.

A **coupon bond** pays periodic interest to the investor between purchase and redemption. Coupon bonds are so named because years ago, investors snipped off small detachable certificates, or coupons, from the bonds and presented the coupons to redeem interest payments from the issuers.

Fortunately the Fonsecas had no junk bonds, Real Estate Investment Trusts (REITs), options, or other types of investments that would have been ill-advised for them. But they also had no plan, and they did not volunteer, nor were they asked, their total financial picture when they invested with each of these four firms. Regrettably, none of the financial professionals had the common sense of our hypothetical roofing contractor. As a result, the Fonsecas' investments were a grab bag. Fortunately, it was a grab bag into which they made deposits, rather than extracting the goodies. In some ways, it was like a Mexican piñata. The problem was that while four investment firms were filling it, it would be Roger and Hazel who would burst it on retirement and try to live on whatever fell out.

Roger had always viewed money as something to save and forget about, and Hazel followed her husband's lead in all matters financial. When he talked to an advisor and complained about paying taxes, the advisor would sell him a tax-free municipal bond fund without inquiring to determine if he really needed tax shelters or was just blowing off steam. More often than not, it was the latter. When he spoke to another broker about low rates of return on his municipal bond funds, the broker would sell him a higher yielding corporate bond fund.

While still working and just beginning to contemplate retirement, Roger was advised to invest for growth. When he mentioned that retirement was imminent, he was told to lighten his exposure to stocks and buy more bond funds. When a stock market correction occurred, he told one of his advisors that he could not tolerate the stress, so the advisor liquidated the stock in the portfolio he controlled. Roger collected brokers the way Jay Leno collects cars, but Roger's collection provided him with far less fun and satisfaction. Lacking a comprehensive knowledge of Roger's finances, the brokers were unable to help him reach his goals.

Part of the problem was that Roger viewed money as a commodity to hoard but not to manage according to a master plan. Over the years, all the advice he received was piecemeal. He probably never gave any one advisor the impression that he had assets beyond his investments with that one advisor, yet he was determined to squeeze recommendations out of all of them. These advisors, who were self-described professionals, never asked about his total investments or, if they did, Roger was not forthcoming.

In spite of this unplanned approach to investing, the Fonsecas managed to amass about $200,000 in the 401(k) account and $160,000 in various mutual funds and brokerage accounts. Their savings would have been far more substantial, however, if they had put a sound asset-allocation plan in place before the bull markets of the 1980s. When we finally met the Fonsecas in 1992, we conducted the meeting in an entirely different way than the brokers and managers Roger had called on over the years. First, we suggested that both Roger and Hazel come to the first meeting. Then we opened that meeting by asking a question that the Fonsecas had never asked of themselves or been asked by any supposed financial professional: "What do you want this money to accomplish for you?"

We then showed them the Financial Physical form (Appendix A) and said that the information called for was essential to our understanding their assets, wants, and needs. "Without this information," we said, "we cannot do a professional job for you. And without a clear understanding of your own situation and goals, all you can do is hurt yourself.

"We would welcome and value the opportunity to work with you and help you," we told the Fonsecas, "but we will not accept you as clients if we cannot help you accomplish your goals. To do that, we need to know your goals and your assets to attain them."

The Fonsecas were stunned. They had never met financial people who did anything but take their money and run.

"Can't you just give us a recommendation?" Roger asked.

"Yes," we said, "our recommendation is that you identify a financial advisor whom you trust and can work with. Stop viewing your savings as a pile of money and start viewing it as a virtual company that needs full-time, professional management. Appoint that manager—us or someone else—and work with him or her to secure your life goals."

Accustomed to being the tailor's customers who were cut to fit the suit, the Fonsecas were pleasantly surprised to discover a tailor who would cut the cloth to their measurements. After a couple of discussions, they overcame their reluctance to share information. The Financial Physical was as revealing an exercise for the Fonsecas as it was for us as their new financial advisors. They had never articulated their desires to each other or drafted financial goals for themselves, so they had never tried to figure out how to attain them, let alone commit them to paper. These discussions revealed that they did not even have a will or any of the other legal documents they might need. Again, no one had ever suggested that they ask themselves the appropriate questions or told them that they might need retirement and estate planning. Relatively ignorant of these processes, they had been reluctant to approach an estate lawyer, fearful that they did not even know what questions to ask.

We told the Fonsecas we would assemble a team of professionals to help them achieve their goals, including an appropriate accountant and lawyer. Again, we asked, "What do you want your money to provide?" As simple as that question sounds—and is—none of their previous advisors or brokers had posed it.

This new way of thinking about saving, investing, and planning led the Fonsecas to contemplate their retirement lifestyle and decide how they wanted to spend it. Since both were physically fit and were skilled home fix-it enthusiasts, they decided to remodel their house.

They also thought they'd enjoy travel. New furniture and, much less important, said Roger, new golf clubs were also on their wish list. They also said they would like to give money to their grandchildren, if they could afford to. At last, we realized we were making progress. A map—a picture of the retirement and the life they envisioned— was taking shape. The Fonsecas had defined realistic, achievable goals. The next step was to determine how to reach those goals. Roger and Hazel were thinking about how much all of their dreams would cost.

First, we knew the Fonsecas had to preview pension and Social Security income to determine how much of their living expenses would be covered by these two sources of income. Both Roger and Hazel were entitled to pensions and Social Security, and a quick analysis confirmed that this fixed income would cover a good deal of day-to-day expenses. Luxuries, on the other hand, would have to be funded by their investment accounts. These included travel, new furniture, and golf clubs.

The Fonsecas were now regarding their investment portfolio not as a collection of savings accounts, but rather as a means to an end. For many years, they had not thought about money as anything more than something to be saved. They collected advisors with no goals or thoughts about the power their savings had, relying on the diversification of investments, even though it was mindless and scattershot, to protect them. Now, they realized that their money could work for them, helping them achieve the goals they were only now bringing into focus. They realized that saving, while essential, was not sufficient. The retirement life they sought was going to cost money, and their investment accounts had to work hard for them.

During the Financial Physical, we reviewed every investment account, mutual fund, and stock and bond one-by-one, asking the Fonsecas the following questions: Why had they made the investment? Why did they still own it? How had it performed? Were they happy with it? What role did it play in the total portfolio? They had few answers, except to say they had tried to be good savers.

With a new outlook, they formed Roger and Hazel Fonseca, Inc. We, as the new COO, began the task of repositioning the portfolio and reallocating the assets. The 401(k) account could be moved to an IRA rollover account at retirement without incurring tax liabilities or penalties. This portion of the portfolio would be reserved for long-term, tax-sheltered growth. Furthermore, since the Fonsecas would not need immediate income from this account, we would have considerable latitude with their taxable income. They could withdraw from the after-tax portfolio to supplement pensions and Social Security.

Roger and Hazel now look upon their investment accounts as a business that requires attention. They realize that the success of this business will determine the quality of their retirement years. They had never realized that their investments had such potential. At our urging, the Fonsecas have not become micromanagers, nor do they spend every waking moment analyzing their account statements line by line. The idea of a virtual business appeals to them, and they function as true CEOs, setting goals, asking questions, and giving direction. Then they let us, as their professional managers, do our job.

As this book goes to press in 2000, the Fonsecas' portfolio is approaching $700,000. They have made withdrawals during the past eight years for vacations, new cars, gifts to grandchildren, and, yes, even for golf clubs. They are enjoying the standard of living they dreamed of when they met us in 1992. They have a computer and trade email and pictures with out-of-state friends and family. They have a good sense of market activity and how it affects their accounts and, in turn, their ability to spend additional dollars.

When the markets become volatile or register a correction, they look forward to conversation and guidance from us. They value the power of advice, not only when the bears growl, but also when the bulls stampede. They take comfort and satisfaction from the ability to discuss their situation with us and the other professionals we have involved in the management of Roger and Hazel Fonseca, Inc. With this guidance, they are confident of their decisions and strategies.

Over the years, the Fonsecas have developed not only a sound business relationship with us, but also a warm personal one. We value them as friends and clients, almost as family for whom we have a fiduciary responsibility. The Fonsecas view us as experienced advisors, friends, consultants, and managers of their family fortune. Their only rebuke has been, "Where were you all those years ago when we needed you?"

Just as we were finishing this chapter, we were profoundly saddened by Hazel's death in her late 60s. We were heartened, however, that, in her final years, she had enjoyed the peace and security that derived from her and Roger's trust in us and from a sensible financial plan they had crafted and were executing with our guidance.

Lessons of Chapter 7

Remember the power of one: To maximize your investment potential, select one trusted financial advisor and work with that person to develop a comprehensive program for your finances. One qualified financial advisor will be more effective in balancing your portfolio than you will be in balancing financial advisors.

Diversification for its own sake does little good and has a huge potential downside. Diversification as part of a comprehensive financial and investment plan minimizes risk and maximizes return. It insulates you from the volatility of the investment markets. But you must provide your financial advisor with a comprehensive picture of your goals, assets, and risk tolerance.

■ ■ ■

Professional's Toolkit

Building Trust With Your Clients

All our experience and all our instincts convince us that the best formula for maximum capital appreciation is for clients to identify a financial advisor whom they trust and enjoy working with. Once they have selected a professional, they should confide without reservation about their goals and total financial circumstances. These circumstances encompass far more than investable assets. They also include earned income, present and expected; sources of fixed income, including pension and Social Security; inheritances on the horizon, dangerous though they are to count on; and relatively illiquid assets, such as real estate and art.

The financial advisor essentially becomes the primary care physician attending to the overall health of the client's virtual business. Like a good primary care physician, the financial advisor needs to recognize when to supplement general knowledge with specialized expertise. In the advisor's case, such expertise may be supplied by an estate planning lawyer, CPA, tax advisor, or insurance agent.

How do you establish client relationships characterized by this kind of confidence and trust? Three ingredients are necessary:

1. You must be worthy of them by virtue of unquestioned integrity, professionalism, and dedication to craft evidenced by, among other factors, lifelong education. If you have no more graduate degrees or certifications than you had five years ago, you're probably not keeping up with your profession.

2. You must take the time and make the effort to elicit information from your clients, and to listen and understand when they respond. The Financial Physical we have developed as Appendix A of this book provides an excellent start.

   This information helps you do the following:

   - Understand what constitutes realistic goals for your clients, how much risk they can tolerate, and what blend of asset classes will help achieve those goals.

   - Identify the professional investment managers who can help reach those goals.

   - Monitor progress and update objectives over time.

   You need to know if your clients want to maximize capital appreciation for the future, produce current income as the primary or secondary goal, or simply avoid long-term capital loss. How soon will your clients need to tap into their investments—in less than three years, three to five years from now, or more than five years hence?

   The Investment Advisers Act of 1940 stipulates your fiduciary duty to act in the client's best interest. The National Association of Securities Dealers and the New York Stock Exchange require registered representatives and broker-dealers to make suitable recommendations to clients. How can you be confident that you are making sensible recommendations in the client's best interest if you do not know that client? You cannot. You must strive to know clients better than they know themselves.

3. Finally, you must realize that no financial advisor is right for every client. Irrespective of your ability, dedication, and good will, some clients will never trust you with their vital information or rely on your counsel. If they ask you to make investments for them based on partial information, you need the integrity and the guts to send those clients, even wealthy ones, elsewhere.

CHAPTER

8

Pitfall 6:
Invest for Immediate Income

"Rule No. 1: Never lose money.
Rule No. 2: Never forget rule No. 1."

—*Warren Buffett*

Thinking Outside the Lines

"Be careful what you ask for," warns the old proverb. "You may just get it."

Too often, financial professionals give clients exactly what they ask for without determining if the clients understand the benefits and risks of the investment instruments they have selected. The clients get what they ask for, but sooner or later regret it.

This does not mean that clients have no say in their investments, or that financial professionals concoct strategies and structure portfolios on their own. It does mean that, when a client says, "I want bonds" or "I want stock in Internet start-up companies," responsible financial professionals do not simply say, "Yes, sir!" or "Yes, ma'am!" They probe the client's reasoning to ensure that the client understands the nature of the investment, its benefits and shortcomings and the risk involved.

For example, many retirees have had it drummed into their heads that they should own bonds or bond funds to provide steady income. They then ask their advisors or brokers to buy whatever bonds provide the highest income. In response, some advisors and brokers may purchase high-yield bonds. These bonds are also called junk bonds and, in our opinion, that term is more accurate. Bonds of any

101

type are often not the most appropriate investment for retirees, and, among bonds, junk bonds are usually the worst choice.

Often, however, retirees have both pensions and Social Security providing a steady, reliable income stream. If the pension is from a large, well-established company, labor union, or public entity, retirees incur virtually no risk in relying on that income rather than bond income.

Many retirees also choose bonds because they think, "Stocks are risky, and bonds are safe." That, too, is a misconception. Jeremy Siegel, professor of finance at the Wharton School of the University of Pennsylvania, writes in the 1998 book *Stocks for the Long Run,* "It is widely known that stock returns, on average, exceed bonds, in the long run. But it is little known that in the long run, the risks in stocks are *less than* those found in bonds or even **bills**! The fact that stocks, in contrast to bonds or bills, have never offered investors a negative real holding period return yield over 20 years or more is also extremely significant. Although it might appear to be riskier to hold stocks than bonds, precisely the opposite is true; the safest long-term investment has clearly been stocks, not bonds." We agree.

> A **Treasury bill** is a certificate representing a short-term loan to the federal government that matures in 3, 6, or 12 months.

Junk bonds do have a place in the investment market. For people who have the wealth to absorb what may be a 100% loss, who understand the risk they are taking, and who make a conscious decision to take it, junk bonds can be an appropriate investment. Some people have made a lot of money investing in junk bonds, and many excellent companies that exist today would not exist if had they not been financed by junk bonds in their formative years. But junk bonds are an extremely high-risk investment and should not constitute a large share of your portfolio—certainly not more than you can afford to lose.

Nina Lambert, the subject of this chapter's first Wealth Story, is an example of someone who got what she asked for in junk bonds and almost lived to regret it.

■ ■ ■

Nina Lambert, Inc.

Gilbert and Nina Lambert lived in Philadelphia and raised three children in middle-class comfort on Gil's income as an optometrist. Nina devoted the first 25 years of their marriage to bearing and raising their three children.

Near their 35th wedding anniversary in the early 1990s, with the children living on their own and the Lamberts in their late 50s, Gil sold his optometry practice and retired. The sale of the optometry practice and their savings provided a retirement portfolio of approximately $450,000. Gil was due to start receiving early retirement benefits from Social Security of about $14,000 per year when he reached age 62. He was also an accomplished jazz pianist who had played in a trio with two friends for years, as a paying avocation. He could earn about $1,200 per month in the trio playing in local nightclubs, and he decided to do so until he reached 62.

Gil and Nina approached a stockbroker who was recommended by their son-in-law, who had been the broker's college roommate. The Lamberts knew nothing about him except that he was their son-in-law's friend. They told him that they wanted to invest their $450,000 in bonds for the maximum steady retirement income. The broker did not inquire about other sources of income, the level of risk they could sustain, or any of the other investment-decision criteria outlined in the early chapters and appendices of this book. He simply took the order and invested the money in U.S. Treasury and blue-chip corporate bonds and investment-grade bond mutual funds, as they directed.

The Lamberts left the broker's office happy and started receiving monthly checks of approximately $2,250. Combined with Gil's paying avocation in the jazz trio, they were living comfortably. Inflation was low in the mid-1990s, so the Lamberts left their investments alone for a couple of years but then decided that a raise in monthly income would be nice. They asked the broker if there were bonds that paid a higher rate of interest. He said there were and shifted about two-thirds of their savings into junk bonds and **closed-end bond** funds traded on the New York Stock Exchange, being careful always to use the term high-yield when he spoke with them. The broker did not fully understand the level of risk to which he was exposing his clients, and he never discussed it with them. Nonetheless, the Lamberts' monthly income increased to a little more than $2,800 per month, and they were again happy. Unfortunately, they were happy in part because they did not understand the level of risk that their request to the stockbroker had incurred for them.

> **Closed-end bond** or mutual funds trade like a stock in that a finite number of shares are issued. There must be a willing buyer to purchase shares when an investor wishes to sell them.

About 18 months later, Gil died suddenly and unexpectedly of a heart attack, depriving Nina of the income she had counted on from his musical avocation. Finding it difficult to live on the monthly payments, Nina called her accountant and explained her predicament. The accountant recommended that Nina and he meet with a qualified investment consultant and financial planner and referred Nina to us, as we had served other clients of his.

We began in the way outlined in this book, completing with her what we call the Financial Physical (Appendix A). At this first meeting, Nina commented that we were asking intelligent, pertinent questions that the stockbroker had never asked Gil or her.

The Financial Physical was reassuring to Nina, but we delivered one piece of alarming news: Nina's $450,000 portfolio had decreased in value to just under $350,000 because several of the companies whose junk bonds she held had gone out of business and several of the closed-end bond funds had traded significantly lower in price due to increases in both interest rates and rates of redemption. We strongly recommended liquidating all junk bonds and closed-end bond fund investments immediately, before they sustained additional losses. We also recommended reinvesting 40% of the $350,000 in investment-grade bonds, 30% in blue-chip value stocks, and 30% in blue-chip growth stocks. The investment-grade bonds would be for income and the stocks for appreciation. That appreciation, we said, would restore the lost money over time and provide a hedge against future inflation. It all made good sense to Nina, and she agreed.

We advised Nina that, to allow the stock portion of the portfolio to grow, she should lower her monthly draw on the portfolio to

$1,750 for at least two to three years. This represented a 6% annual draw on her investments, which was higher than we preferred, but Nina had no choice. She needed the money to live on. Nina understood why even the reduced payments of $1,750 were stretching the boundaries of prudence, and she was able to get by on that income.

We explained to Nina the benefits of taking a **reverse mortgage** on her condominium, which she and Gil had paid off fully, as a way to increase her monthly income without invading the portfolio. Nina was reluctant to do so, for reasons partly logical and partly emotional. On an emotional level, owning the home gave her a sense of security. We explained that the reverse mortgage guaranteed her the right to live in the condo until death, but our explanations did not mollify her. On a logical level, she wanted to be able to leave it to her children to sell for her grandchildren's college educations. We pointed out that her children were responsible, self-sufficient adults who had their own financial situations in good order. We reminded her that the children had repeatedly said, "We're okay, Mom, and don't need the condo when you die. We want you to be happy and secure." She understood this, but still wanted to leave them the real estate.

> In a **reverse mortgage,** a bank, insurance company, or other financial services firm purchases the clear title, that is one not carrying a mortgage or other encumbrances, to a residence. The seller remains a resident for his or her natural life, receiving monthly payments in return for the title. Upon the resident's death, the financial services company sells the property.

The advisability of the reverse mortgage was a discussion point at each annual review. We would say to Nina, "As stubborn as you can be in resisting our advice of a reverse mortgage, we can be just as stubborn in continuing to recommend it."

Nina appreciated our candor, recognizing we were speaking in what she believed was her best interest, but she refused to give in. Then, in late 1999, good fortune intervened. Nina received a windfall inheritance of about $50,000 from an uncle who, as it turned out, had saved more money than any of his relatives had realized, and bequeathed more money than they had anticipated. Added to her now appreciating portfolio, that gave her a total nest egg of approximately $435,000 at the outset of 2000, enabling her to stay in the condo with no reverse mortgage and no financial imposition on her children. Her monthly income of $1,750, sufficient for the present, was now 4.8% of her portfolio. We said this was a more prudent withdrawal and strongly advised that Nina not increase her draw. Since she had been able to get by on that amount, she agreed.

With intelligent investing and a continued strong stock market, Nina may be able to give herself raises in three to five years. This will enable her income to keep pace with, if not exceed, inflation. Aside from missing Gil and the retirement life together that they had anticipated, she is content and, by her definition, wealthy.

Lesson: A financial consultant who is doing the best job for you will not simply carry out your decision to invest in junk bonds or any other instrument without fully explaining to you how it works and the risk involved. A good professional financial advisor will expend the effort to understand your financial situation and lifestyle goals and will work with you on an individual basis, presenting several alternatives to reach as many of those goals as your financial resources allow.

Irwin and Elaine Pollack, Inc.

Irwin and Elaine Pollack got what they asked for from their stockbroker. Unfortunately that included not one, but two, ill-advised (for them) investment vehicles: junk bonds and **limited partnerships.**

A **limited partnership** is an investment in a business that typically earns a fixed payment that is made before the general partners receive any share in the profits, but that confers no vote in the conduct of the business. In many cases, the appeal of limited partnerships to investors is a promised tax advantage. Often, however, investors fail to realize that many limited partnerships have a limited secondary market. This means that if investors want to sell their shares, they may not be able to do so or may be forced to accept pennies on the dollar. Because of this, limited partnerships should be considered an extremely illiquid investment.

When Irwin retired from his lifelong managerial position with a women's garment manufacturer in the mid-1980s, he and Elaine decided to sell their large Colonial home in an affluent suburb of New York City and enjoy the good life on the golf courses of Florida's gold coast. They purchased a much smaller but luxurious condominium in a palm tree-filled country club development and added the profit to their portfolio. Once settled in their new community, the Pollacks thought it would be prudent to transfer the oversight of their investments to a local stockbroker, bringing with them a substantial portfolio of about $750,000 in tax-deferred CDs. They asked the new broker to invest the funds for maximum monthly income, and they volunteered no information about the level of risk with which they were comfortable. Worse, the broker never asked. She simply gave them what they asked for with no questions or discussion, sinking their savings into junk bonds and limited partnerships. This yielded a monthly income of approximately $5,600. For a time, the Pollacks were happy with what they had asked for.

One of us met Irwin on the golf course in Florida in November 1994. My wife and I were visiting relatives, who happened to live in the condo next to the Pollacks. During the course of the week, Irwin and I hit it off, discovering that we shared a similar sense of humor in addition to a passion for the links. Just after I returned to the office, I got a call from Irwin, who wanted to share a great joke. He then asked if I would be willing to review his and Elaine's portfolio.

Unfortunately there was no humor in what their portfolio assessment revealed. Interest rates had risen throughout the year, the value of their junk bonds had fallen correspondingly, and several of the companies whose junk bonds they held had gone out of business. But the bad news did not stop there.

I also informed the Pollacks that their limited partnerships were extremely illiquid, meaning there was no active trading market for them, so the Pollacks could not sell them. Even if they could have sold them, it would have been at a substantial discount, possibly sacrificing as much as 80% to 90% of their original investment. This is a characteristic of limited partnerships that the broker should have explained to the Pollocks, but did not. As stated earlier, she simply did what they asked—she invested for the highest possible monthly income. Limited partnerships are sophisticated, long-term investments that can be appropriate for wealthy investors who understand their nature and can afford to wait years to reap their financial reward. People in the Pollacks' circumstances should not, in our view, invest in limited partnerships. Once we explained these instruments to the Pollacks, as their previous broker should have before their money was allocated, they agreed.

By this time, the original $750,000 had declined to approximately $630,000. The Pollacks were well on their way from comfort and security to concern and worry. They immediately formed Irwin and Elaine Pollack, Inc., and appointed us COO. We began by investing $480,000 in investment-grade municipal bonds paying 5.5% to 8.75% interest tax-free. We invested the remaining $150,000 in tax-deferred variable annuities of $75,000 each. One was owned by Irwin and the other by Elaine. We did this not only in hopes of increasing the principle through tax-deferred growth, but because of the sense of security the annuities offered with the death benefit guarantee and annual step-up. These annuities invested in common stocks—one-third each in international growth, mid-cap U.S. growth, and blue-chip growth stocks.

After this reinvestment, the Pollacks received $1,000 per month from the annuities ($500 each) and $3,000 per month from the bonds. This represented a decrease in income from their previous asset allocation, but it provided the security they needed, immediately and for the long term. The Pollacks were able to live on the reduced income and agreed that the enhanced security more than compensated for the decrease in spending money. We told them that, if their portfolio appreciated as expected, they would be able to restore income over time. We also brought on board a new CPA, who recognized that the Pollacks' losses from the sale of the junk bonds and, eventually, from the limited partnerships, provided the opportunity for tax-loss carryforwards, which eliminated the Pollacks' income tax for three to four years.

Over the next few years, as some of the municipal bonds matured, interest rates dropped and the stock market soared. For these reasons, we invested $25,000 from matured bonds into Irwin's equities-based annuity. The surging stock market enabled us to boost the annuity income gradually but steadily during the next few years from $1,000 per month to $1,750. Even with these increased withdrawals, the Pollacks' original variable annuity portfolio of $175,000 (the original $150,000 deposit plus an additional deposit of $25,000) appreciated to almost $500,000 by the end of 1999.

As this book goes to press, the Pollacks are in their early 80s with financial security for the rest of their lives. In 1998, they sold their Florida retirement house for a substantial gain, bought a less expensive condominium where all maintenance and lawn care are the responsibility of the management company, and invested $150,000 in a conservative growth fund for their children. The annual income from the Pollacks' investments has rebounded to $60,000, and they don't spend all of that. Elaine is so sensible about her expenditures for household needs that she actually saves about $10,000 per year from the $60,000 in spending money.

Occasionally, Irwin calls me and after presenting his newest joke, asks for a raise—a little extra spending money. In these cases, I ask to speak to Elaine, and I inquire about how much she has accumulated in their savings and checking account. When relentless questioning reveals, as it invariably does, that she has squirreled away $5,000 to $15,000, often in a checking account earning no interest, I ask, "Elaine, do you want to increase your tax liabilities?" She says, "No," and I say, "Irwin wants some money for (whatever it is). Please give it to him from the checking account." Elaine typically counters that they "cannot afford it," but she knows they can and eventually relents.

This is a little game among Irwin, Elaine, and me. It may sound silly to some, but it is rooted in love and a concern for the future. And in the end, it works out well for both Irwin and Elaine, who are enjoying each other's love and companionship, along with financial security, in their elder years.

Lesson: Your financial advisor should not give you what you ask for without ensuring that you understand fully the characteristics, advantages, and shortcomings of the investment vehicles—in short, how those investments will affect your life.

Lessons of Chapter 8

Be specific with your financial advisor about your income needs and financial goals, rather than about the types of investments you think you need. You may not be aware of all the characteristics, risks, and long-term effects of those investments. A candid discussion with your financial advisor will enable him or her to develop a strategy and comprehensive plan to achieve your goals, and will give you the opportunity to understand fully the recommended investment types.

Be suspicious of financial advisors who simply execute your orders and do not explain the risks and effects on your portfolio.

■ ■ ■

Professional's Toolkit

Investing in Bonds

The first question to ask retired clients who think they need bonds for fixed income is, "Do you have other sources of fixed income?" Consider a fixed annual income of $24,000 that a client derives from a pension and Social Security. For your client to earn that income from a bond portfolio, with a comparable degree of safety and reliability, the client would need a portfolio of approximately $400,000 in long-term, non-callable bonds from the U.S. Treasury or blue-chip corporations, paying annual interest of 6%.

You may find that many investors overlook two critical aspects of bond risk, the first of which is inflation. Let's say your client is holding a substantial portion of savings in safe, noncallable, long-term bonds. By safe bonds, we mean those issued by organizations that will not default on their obligations, such as the U.S. Treasury or blue-chip corporations—preferably those rated AAA by Standard & Poor's and Moody's. Let's further posit that those bonds are paying 6.5% interest. As long as inflation remains at the level of the late 1990s, less than 5%, your client is making money. But as recently as the late 1970s, the United States experienced double-digit inflation. If inflation rises to 8%, for example, your client will be earning 6.5% on paper, but, taking into account the effects of inflation, losing 1.5 percent, *before* accounting for the taxes to be paid.

The second aspect of bond risk that is often overlooked is the relationship between bond value and interest rates. As interest rates increase, bond value decreases, and the reverse is also true. Let's say we are in a period of rising interest rates, and a fictitious client, Lorraine Travis, needs to sell some bonds for unexpected expenses or an extraordinary purchase. She will be unpleasantly surprised to find that she must sell them for less than face value.

Now let's assume the opposite happens. Interest rates drop and some of Lorraine's bonds that have been paying 6.5% mature. She has become accustomed to receiving that return on her principle and has been living at the level that income will support. When the bonds mature, Lorraine redeems them, but when she replaces them with new bonds, she can earn only 5.75%. On an investment of $200,000 in bonds, she finds that she earns $1,500 less per year on her principle. Another way of looking at it is that Lorraine has just suffered an 11.5% pay cut on this portion of her investments.

High-yield bonds, also called junk bonds, have these risks and a huge additional danger. These bonds are issued by shaky corporations and pay higher interest rates than safer bonds because of their risk. The companies may go out of business, declare bankruptcy, and default on their obligations. You may encounter unsophisticated investors who are seduced by those high rates without realizing the attendant risk.

Bonds can be an important part of a client's portfolio, especially for a client who does not have a steady pension and Social Security. In particular, short-term bonds are a good solution for a client to maintain ample liquidity. There are inherent pros and cons to bonds, and it depends on your individual client's needs and goals whether they are appropriate. As with all investment instruments, you should discuss the associated risks when recommending bonds to your client.

Male Investors Are From Mars; Female Investors Are From Venus

"We women ought to put first things first. Why should we mind if men have their faces on the money, as long as we get our hands on it?"
—Ivy Baker Priest

Women Are Successful Investors

With so much emphasis being placed on the sociological differences between men and women, we were curious if there were differences in investing styles between the sexes. As a starting point, we examined our own client base, looking for patterns and traits unique to males or females. What we discovered was that among our clientele, females who managed the investment relationship were some of the most successful of our clients in achieving their goals. Thinking about how our women clients handle their finances, we had our own theories about why so many were such successful investors. Our research of published studies on this topic bore out our conclusions.

In short, we observed four major reasons that many women are so successful in managing their finances. First, in our experience, female investors typically invest their energy in establishing a comfortable relationship with us as their financial planners, and then trust us to go ahead and implement the plan we develop. Second, women generally invest less of their ego in financial decision-making, which gives them the ability to relinquish control of the implementation of their plan. This enables them to focus more energy on other areas of their lives. A third common trait that successful female investors share is the patience to let the plan go to work for them long-term. As we've discussed in other chapters in this book, investors who stick with a plan for the long term tend to be more financially rewarded than those who constantly insist on shifting focus. Finally, women are generally more disciplined at saving money in their investment accounts than men. Many women say that the fact that they typically earn less than men creates a greater urgency for them to save and invest.

Establishing a Partnership With the Financial Advisor

Indeed, a 1999 PaineWebber study of women investing more than $100,000 and their investing patterns revealed that most women investors have strong partnerships with their financial advisors (Figure 9.1). Even in the Internet age, one-third of the 900 women who were interviewed for the study said they rely on advice from financial professionals. Because women traditionally earn less than men, conventional wisdom suggests that many women investors believe they are treated less seriously by financial advisors. Yet in reality, the study showed that 73% of the women investors polled work with financial advisors and they said that maintaining strong partnerships with their advisors is important.

The Importance of Understanding the Financial Plan

In our experience, most women investors want a detailed explanation of the strategy we lay out in their plan. However, once they have a solid understanding, they feel confident enough with the direction that they do not feel the need to know all the specifics of implementation. Often highly skilled at balancing a career and motherhood, many female investors have learned the importance of delegation of duties. They spend the time up front evaluating and selecting the most capable professional to handle their account. Then they outline their goals and work with their advisor to develop a plan to reach those goals. During this process, they build a relationship based on trust and mutual understanding. They then achieve a level of comfort that allows them to rely on the professional to reach the designated goals. By contrast, many men tend to microfocus and challenge the details. They need to feel ownership not only of the plan, but also of the execution. Sometimes, unfortunately, this results in the derailment of the plan.

Have a financial advisor?

Yes	73%
No, but need one	4%

Relationship with financial advisor:

Good partnership with advisor	91%
Advisor acts as sounding board	79%
Good recommendations from advisor	90%
Advisor takes lead	72%
Get better performance with advisor	82%

How advisor is used:

Order taker	10%
Respondent takes initiative, advisor reviews	27%
Advisor takes initiative, respondent reviews	46%
Advisor mostly does everything	15%

FIGURE 9.1 Financial Advisor Relationships
Women and Investing II ©1999 PaineWebber, Incorporated.

Just as many lost male drivers adamantly refuse to ask for directions, many male investors are reluctant to ask for clarification about financial concepts. Women are typically not embarrassed to ask questions, and they take their education process seriously, using all available outlets. According to the PaineWebber study, women frequently use technology in the investing process, yet fewer than 5%, on average, reported that they use the Internet to actually execute trades. They take the initiative in educating themselves about their finances, and, once they are satisfied that they have a solid understanding, they are able to commit to the plan.

Confirming our experience, a 1992 article in *Money* cited the top reason that women are often smarter than men about money is the fact that "they admit it when they don't know something." In addition, the article disclosed that women are not afraid to seek professional help with their finances, they avoid risk, they do their homework, and they set goals.

Developing a Financial Identity

How common is it for women to have control of their financial and investment decision-making? More common than conventional

A way to achieve financial independence	76%
Good performance in the markets	73%
In charge of family finances	68%
Always expected to do their own investing	59%
Want to leave a legacy	57%
Inspired by someone to take charge	52%
Raised to think about investments	50%
Retired	35%
Major breadwinner in household	35%
Received an inheritance	33%
Changed marital status	29%

FIGURE 9.2 Reasons Women Have Taken Control of Their
Investment Decision-Making
"Women and Investing II" ©1999 Paine Webber, Incorporated

wisdom suggests. The PaineWebber study revealed that 93% of respondents were involved in the process, with more than 75% saying their primary reason for investing was to achieve financial independence. (Figure 9.2 reveals the other reasons women are involved in the process.) What's more, two-thirds of women polled maintain investment accounts separate from their spouses.

Following are Wealth Stories of three of our successful women clients. They all share four important traits: the desire to develop a trusting partnership with their advisor; the confidence that they are in control of their finances, even though they are not handling the implementation firsthand; a keen ability to save; and the commitment to stick to the plan.

□ □ □

Virginia Sewell, Inc.

We had known Ginny Sewell as a voice on the telephone for 10 years before she came to us as a client. Ginny was a legal secretary at a firm in New London, Connecticut, working for two estate attorneys with whom we occasionally did business. Her extreme efficiency in handling legal matters was only surpassed by her sincere friendliness in our telephone dealings over the years. Months would pass between phone calls, but Ginny would always remember to ask about the events and milestones in our families, taking genuine interest and following up especially if someone had been ill. The affable voice on the other end of the phone defied Ginny's actual age, so we were quite surprised when she told us early in 1996 that she would be turning 65 in June of that year and would retire from the firm.

Widowed for more than 30 years, Ginny was frightened about the prospect of leaving the working world. She confessed to us that she did not know much about investing and was concerned about generating enough income and maintaining the principal. Having known us for years, Ginny said she had developed trust in our relationship and confidence in us as financial planners, and asked us to help her plan the next stage in her financial life. She told us that she wanted us to take the lead in developing a program for her to follow. While she wanted to understand the strategy we would put in place, she did not want to be bogged down in the details of implementing it. We were honored and eagerly agreed to work with her.

Ginny had participated fully in the 401(k) plan that the law firm offered. At retirement, her $125,000 in the 401(k) plan was split among various bond funds and stock funds. While she had saved religiously in her retirement plan, according to Ginny, she had made the investment choices within the plan by "throwing a dart." While she did not have the most strategic allocation plan, at least Ginny had had the discipline to stick with investment choices. Over the long term, this discipline typically is more profitable than the opposite extreme of chasing the market and shifting investments too often.

The second component of Ginny's portfolio was a series of bond funds totaling $75,000. The third and final piece of the portfolio was a fixed-rate annuity of about $150,000 that was paying between 5% and 6%, which she had funded with an inheritance she had received from an uncle 10 years previously.

Ginny talked to us candidly about her lifestyle and investment goals. She would be receiving $15,000 annually in Social Security and pension income. She had no mortgage on her small, impeccably maintained home, as she had paid it off 15 years before. Her only child, a son, was running a very successful business overseas and would not need her financial support. Ginny was looking forward to spending more time with the crafting club she had belonged to since her husband died. She had developed invaluable friendships with the other women in the club over the years and envisioned filling her free time creating beautiful quilts and traveling to regional craft fairs with her companions. After reviewing her spending needs, Ginny told us she would be comfortable with a monthly income of $2,000.

When we sat down with Ginny several weeks later to present our recommendations, we put aside the entire afternoon, as we knew she wanted to understand fully the rationale behind the strategy. The first issue we discussed was achieving her income requirement. We recommended moving the $150,000 in fixed annuities to variable annuities, explaining the need for growth of assets. We selected a mix of stock funds, both U.S. and global. This would provide the $750 per month supplement to the Social Security and pension income, giving Ginny the $2,000 per month she had requested.

The next portion of the portfolio that we discussed was the bond funds. We explained that we advised moving this money to a conservative portfolio, which had a balance of bond funds, large-cap stock funds, and small- and mid-cap stock funds. We would rely on a computer model to allocate the $75,000 among these funds, based on Ginny's answers to a number of questions. These funds would have more growth than if we kept them solely invested in bonds and yet would be invested for relatively low risk. In addition, the portfolio would be completely liquid, enabling Ginny to make withdrawals in case she required more income or had special spending needs.

Finally, the 401(k) funds needed to be rolled over into an IRA. We recommended to Ginny a core-equity conservative-value portfolio manager, who would invest for longer-term growth over the next five years until she was required to begin making withdrawals at age 70½.

In response to Ginny's questions, we provided a more detailed explanation of investment markets and vehicles, being careful not to become too technical. We told Ginny that we insisted on meeting with her annually to review performance and any changes in her needs. In the interim, we were just a phone call away. We encouraged her to call us anytime she had questions or needed a reminder of why we had structured her portfolio in this particular way. We reminded her that we were still those guys who had developed a relationship with her on the phone, and we intended to continue that relationship.

During the first two or three market corrections that Ginny encountered with her new plan in place, she was understandably a bit panicked. She never hesitated to call us to talk about the situation, and we continually and patiently explained what was happening. We reminded her that she was positioned for long-term profitability and, at the end of our conversations, she inevitably felt comfortable that we were on the right track.

Four years later, Ginny has stuck with the plan (true to her investment history), and has reaped the benefits. As she had dreamed, she spent much of the first two years of her retirement devoted entirely to her crafting hobby. In fact, she developed such a dear friendship with the owner of a small craft supply shop near her home, that two years ago she began working there part-time to keep herself busy two days a week. Although Ginny doesn't need the money, she earns an additional $6,000 per year, bringing her annual income to about $30,000. She enjoys the work tremendously, and the shop owner has told her that she may continue her part-time employment as long as she likes.

Ginny has been fortunate not to need to dip into the balanced fund, which we had invested as a liquid asset if she ever needed it. The fund has earned about 11% per year, bringing its current value to $115,000. Her IRA portfolio has grown from $125,000 to $225,000. We estimate that next year she will probably have to take distributions of between $11,000 and $13,000.

Ginny is the epitome of a successful investor. She is in control of her financial plan, yet she delegates the execution of the details to a professional. She conscientiously follows the market and its effects on her investments, but she has the discipline to adhere to her plan. She meets with us regularly and looks to us for counsel and comfort during market corrections. In short, she is keenly interested in—but not obsessed with—her finances.

Allyson Lindsay, Inc.

Herb and Pauline Lindsay had been clients of ours for about four years, when they asked us at their annual portfolio review meeting if we would be willing to help their daughter, who had recently started out in the working world. Their daughter, Allyson, had graduated magna cum laude from Northwestern University in Chicago two years before, in 1990, and had stayed in the Windy City to take a job as an assistant account executive at a major advertising agency. Herb and Carol proudly described Allyson as an exceedingly hardworking, focused, organized young woman, who could benefit substantially in the long term from establishing a financial plan so early in her career. Music to our ears!

We wholeheartedly agreed with her parents' assessment of Allyson at our first meeting and added to their list words like professional, intelligent, and self-directed. In her two years at the advertising agency, Allyson had quickly risen in the ranks to a senior account executive, and it was easy to see why. At 24, she possessed charisma and diplomacy well beyond her years, coupled with a positive attitude toward solving problems. She was clearly someone with a promising career ahead of her.

Allyson admitted that she was relieved to find at our first meeting that we were only about 10 years older than she. She had envisioned her parents' financial planners as "older, intimidating gentlemen" with no pulse on the issues her generation faced. We told her about our experience as financial planners, and Allyson shared her aspirations for her own advertising career. She admitted she was sheepish at the amount of investable money she had, but we assured her that the important fact was not the amount of money, but the decision to invest. We explained to her the benefit of investing at such a young age and the power of compounding. We talked with her about setting up a plan and having the discipline to adhere to it. Allyson told us that in her few years in the advertising industry, she had grown to value relationships with clients who agreed on a direction and then allowed her to go on her own course to achieve the results. She said that she wanted to be that kind of client to us, since it would give her the time to focus on her own career. Comfortable with our new relationship, Allyson funded her investment portfolio with $4,000, divided evenly among four stock funds. We also helped her allocate the money in her 401(k) account among several stock funds. Then, taking pains not to sound like the crusty old codgers she had feared us to be, we took the opportunity to give her our best older-brotherly advice for the younger investor: Save, save, save!

And save she did. Every month, Allyson would mail in a portion of her growing paycheck for her stock accounts, and she routinely saved the majority of her annual bonuses. Every few months, we would give her an encouraging phone call to emphasize how proud we were to see her accounts growing so steadily. She would tell us how enriching her career was becoming and how thankful she was to have us monitoring her finances so she could focus fully on her clients. Allyson was motivated to save by knowing that the more she put away now, the less she'd need to save later. She also strived to set up her investments at a young age, so she would have the freedom and comfort in ten years to work fewer hours, and consequently earn less, when she might be raising a family. Goal-oriented by nature, Allyson aimed at building her portfolio to $125,000, at which point we would be able to invest $100,000 with a private money manager and maintain the rest in a liquid account.

Within five years, Allyson had become a vice president at the agency and was earning more than $100,000 annually. She purchased the condominium in the high-rise building she had lived in since she graduated from Northwestern at the bargain price of $125,000. Her landlords, an older couple who lived on the floor above, adored Allyson as a tenant and neighbor, and because they thought of her as a daughter, they offered it to her below market value.

At our review meeting with Allyson last fall, we had the pleasure of informing her that, at age 32, she had reached her $125,000 goal. This milestone accomplishment enabled us to invest $100,000 with a private money manager in an aggressive-growth, high-P/E blue-chip fund. As we go to press, the account has increased in value to $125,000. Additionally, Allyson has about $25,000 in money-market assets, which she uses for bill-paying and daily expenses. Her 401(k) account value is more than $150,000, and she has $25,000 of equity in her condo. By saving and adding to what Allyson classified as a "measly $4,000" eight years ago, her net worth is now $325,000!

At the meeting, we illustrated for Allyson the power of her long-term growth plan and diligent savings from a young age. We told her that if, from that moment on, she never saved another penny, and her investments grew at 12% per year for the next 18 years, at age 50 she would have a portfolio worth $2.3 million. And assuming the same rate of return for the five years following, her portfolio would total more than $4 million at age 55. But if she did indeed decide to continue adding $10,000 in savings per year to the portfolio, she would amass $5.2 million at age 55.

We've asked Allyson her secret to being so successful at a young age. She modestly attributes it to her ability to delegate and stay empassioned about the things that matter to her most: staying close with her family and friends and making sure her clients are happy.

Diana Marsh and Ian McGillivray, Inc.

It was easy to see that Diana and Ian were truly in love when one of us met them ten years ago. My wife and I were the only two waiting to take a tour of one of the oldest champagne cellars in Epernay, France, when another couple hurried in, asking if they had missed the afternoon tour. Delighted to have arrived in time, Diana and Ian were even more pleased to find that the two other people on the tour were also Americans. Our afternoon together exploring the history and production of the precious bubbles revealed that Diana and Ian were newlyweds, escaping to France on a much-needed, restful honeymoon.

In their early 30s, both Diana and Ian were self-described workaholics. Diana was a television news reporter for the top network affiliate in New York City, and Ian managed an executive search firm in Westchester County. Underscoring what a small world it is, we discovered that Diana and my wife had graduated from the same college several years apart and shared some of the same favorite professors. In addition, we found that we were staying at the same hotel in Paris and all had a penchant for classic French cuisine. At the end of the afternoon, after toasting to our newfound friendship, we made plans to meet for dinner in Paris two nights later.

An indescribable gastronomic experience, that dinner cemented our friendship. We shared stories of our careers and our childhoods, our families and our dreams. We ate and drank and laughed so much that we knew we would see each other again back in the States.

So I was not surprised, after getting back to the office, to get a call from Diana. After revisiting our culinary orgy, Diana addressed the point of her call. Since their trip, she and Ian had been discussing the fact that they needed a financial planner. They had realized that with their newly pooled assets, mostly CDs, they had more than $1 million. As Diana had more interest in managing the finances than Ian, they had decided that she would be the decision-maker. Diana wanted me to work with her to develop a plan for saving and investing. Flattered, I agreed.

Without any tangible goal in mind except to maximize the return on her and Ian's savings, Diana had me help her set up a strategy. We determined when each CD would mature and set out to ease slowly into equities. Respecting Diana's comfort level, we developed a program that had a small component, 20%, in U.S. Treasury bonds, with the rest in equities. After understanding the fundamentals of Modern Portfolio Theory, Diana agreed to rely on this formula to allocate the equity portion of the portfolio. We invested in a mix of U.S. and international private money managers with various styles of investment.

Diana was a disciplined investor. She diligently made sure that she and Ian saved their annual bonus checks, adding them to the growing portfolio. She eventually told me that their goal was to have financial independence, so if they wanted to give up their careers, they could do so while maintaining their lifestyle. When I asked her how much money it would take for them to live comfortably, Diana laughed. She said she had never thought about an exact figure, but joked, "I'd say $400,000 of annual income could go a long way to making me happy."

Within three years, Diana was called up by the network to be the on-air correspondent at one of the major posts in Washington, DC. She and Ian adjusted to spending the weekdays apart and relished their weekends together. Even with the added responsibility and tremendous time constraints of her new position, Diana never gave up her role as financial decision-maker. She met with me yearly to reëvaluate the plan, and always left the meeting with a renewed commitment to executing it successfully.

Ian's career was also going well. With successive promotions, Ian was working on highly lucrative deals, placing top-level officers at technology companies. He was able to relocate to Washington, DC and work from an office in the beautiful home they bought in a Virginia suburb.

Then in 1995, a dream came true for Diana and Ian when their daughter Isabelle was born. Diana took several months off from work to spend with her newborn, and then returned to her network position. Ian then became the stay-at-home parent, combining childcare responsibilities with about 30 hours of work per week out of his home office.

Shortly after Diana returned to work, I suggested to her that she and Ian think about developing an estate plan. She was extremely receptive to the idea. I introduced her to an estate attorney with whom we do much business, and we collaborated on a plan that we designed to protect assets for Isabelle, since the portfolio was doing so well. Diana and Ian appointed guardians for Isabelle and created a trust vehicle for her in the case of their untimely death.

Rounding out her team of financial advisors, Diana has brought her own tax accountant into the mix. She has fostered a working relationship between the members of her financial team, and she encourages us to work together on her financial matters, especially during tax season. She trusts that we are all working in her best interest and makes sure we are all on track by organizing periodic teleconferences.

Over the years, when I have deemed it prudent to add managers to Diana and Ian's portfolio, I have called Diana and explained to her the rationale behind my recommendation. Inevitably, after a short discussion, she agrees and requests that I send her the appropriate paperwork. She doesn't agonize over these issues; she has come to value my judgment and she has unwavering confidence in her own ability as a decision-maker.

Diana's commitment to the plan we developed ten years ago has paid off. At this year's review meeting, I informed her and Ian that the portfolio is now worth $8 million. I reminded Diana of her goal of saving enough to live comfortably off the income. While Diana adores her highly visible, well-paying job and has no plans to leave it, I informed her that she and Ian could pack up Isabelle and run off to Tahiti tomorrow, because 5% withdrawals from their portfolio would provide the $400,000 per year she had joked about needing to retire in comfort. Proud of their accomplishments, Diana and Ian committed to forge ahead with the same plan in place, and vowed to update their estate plan in light of their substantially increased net worth.

As treasured friends throughout the years, we felt there was only one way to celebrate appropriately this milestone. Coming full circle from the memorable dinner in Paris, my wife joined us to toast a bottle of fine champagne over an extraordinary meal at one of the Capital's most exceptional restaurants.

Lessons of Chapter 9

Work hard up front to evaluate and select a financial advisor whom you trust. Don't be afraid to ask questions to learn about the investing process. Take ownership of your financial plan, but have enough confidence in your advisor that you are able to relinquish the detailed implementation of the plan. Be a disciplined saver. Evaluate your plan annually with your advisor, and don't hesitate to call with any interim issues you feel are important to achieving your goals.

■ ■ ■

Professional's Toolkit

Working With Female Clients

Working with women investors requires a unique approach both in terms of investment strategy and client service. With a life expectancy seven years longer than men, on average, women will need to save more money than men over their lifetimes. At the same time, says a report in *Fortune* (3/29/99), relatively few women qualify for pensions because they tend to hold service-sector jobs, work for small companies, or drop in and out of the workforce. Those who do earn pensions receive on average only half as much as men. So in the end, women wind up living longer but with less money to live on.

Even though women need larger nest eggs, however, they tend to be more conservative investors. Recent information from a survey by Oppenheimer Funds reveals that many advisors simply assume women are more conservative and sell them government bonds. "What they really should have been doing was encouraging women to be more aggressive," points out Oppenheimer CEO Bridget Macaskill.

According to a study by the National Center for Research at Long Island University, a growing number of women understand that educating themselves about money allows them to make financial decisions without anxiety. In the process they get a feeling of control, security and freedom. Spending the time with female clients to listen to and address their concerns is critical. Be accessible, be patient, be thorough, because you play an important role in the education of your female clients. And most importantly, don't be condescending. Make sure the woman client knows she is in control of her plan and that you operate together as a partnership. Armed with knowledge about her portfolio and trust in you as the financial advisor, the female investor is empowered to adhere to her plan, which can result in better returns for her over the long term.

PART
3

Preserving Wealth

CHAPTER 1

You've Made It.
Now Spend It, Save It, or Give It Away

"I'm proud to be paying taxes in the United States. The only
thing is—I could be just as proud for half the money."
—Arthur Godfrey

The Benefits of Estate Planning

Estate planning may not have the distinguished lineage of the stock
market, which some people trace to the agora of ancient Greece, but
it is certainly not a twentieth-century invention. As early as the six-
teenth century, English landowners devised ways to transfer property titles to third parties while retaining some of the benefits of
ownership. Thus was born the concept behind today's trust agreement, an important instrument of modern estate planning.

What is estate planning? It is the process by which you and your
family arrange for the distribution of everything you own after your
death. Estate planning has three goals: (1) To minimize estate
expenses and taxes; (2) To prepay those expenses so your heirs are
not forced to come up with the money when you die; and (3) To ensure that assets remaining after estate fees and taxes (the government grabs its share first) are distributed in a timely, orderly way
according to your wishes.

Tax minimization is one of the most important benefits of estate
planning. If you are one who regularly complains about income
taxes, FICA taxes, capital gains taxes, property taxes, sales taxes,
and other taxes, consider this: For a steadily growing number of

people, estate taxes will probably be the largest single tax bill they ever owe.

"So what? I won't be around to worry about it," you may think. That is true, but without estate planning on your part, your children, grandchildren, other relatives, friends and business associates, alma maters, favorite charities, and others may be unnecessarily deprived of bequests you would like them to receive. They may even have to liquidate assets to pay the taxes on them. In fact, two NFL franchises, the Miami Dolphins and Washington Redskins, have changed hands in recent years for this reason. But you don't have to inherit something this valuable to be forced to sell it to pay estate taxes. Many children of farmers and ranchers have been forced to sell the family spreads when their parents die, losing not only their homes and the businesses in which they have invested their lives, but also their way of life.

Under the law as this book goes to press, estate taxes are due in full within nine months of the estate owner's death—no extensions. Any delays result in penalties equal to 5% of the money owed for each late month, plus additional interest charges.

The Cost of No Estate Planning

How serious are the problems caused by a lack of estate planning? Very serious. Your heirs will be left with three options for payment: using their own cash, borrowing cash, or selling inherited assets. If your heirs are forced to sell stocks in a bear market to cover estate taxes, they may receive far less than if they had the option to hold the securities for just a few years. If they must sell bonds before maturity as interest rates are rising, which depresses bond prices, they may receive far less than they should. They may be forced to sell a family business just as it has lost its founding partner, discouraging buyers and depressing the price. Liquidating inherited IRAs, 401(k) plan assets, or pension accounts will result in substantial federal and state taxes, depriving your heirs of a patrimony expected by both generations.

Such situations are easily avoidable, however, as basic estate planning is a relatively short, simple process. It requires a limited effort on your part and competent financial planning and estate law advice. The latter is provided by a lawyer specializing in the field.

Drawing Up a Last Will and Testament

Step one in estate planning is executing a will, professionally and expertly drawn by a lawyer and updated as your financial and life circumstances change. Figure 10.1 lists various assets that you should consider including in a will. If you already have one, you may find that it's so outdated that it still provides for guardianship of your now adult children. In the absence of a will, a state court will appoint a lawyer or fiduciary to handle the estate, driving up estate fees. For one thing, that fiduciary's fees will be paid from your estate before your heirs receive a nickel. Your family may even have to post a bond with the court, and your surviving spouse may receive a diminished inheritance.

It is widely legal for you to write your own will, and the forms and formats are readily available in how-to books and on Websites. However, we strongly recommend retaining a qualified, experienced estate lawyer to write your will, especially if you will need a more complex estate plan, with trusts and other instruments. As part of the Economic Recovery Tax Act of 1981, Congress created the Unlimited Marital Deduction, enabling a husband and wife to pass all their assets from the one who dies first to the survivor with no inheritance tax obligation. The Unified Marital Deduction leads many married couples to believe that a simple will is all they need. After all, the husband and wife can provide for each other with no inheritance tax obligation. But the Unified Marital Deduction only postpones probate and inheritance taxes; it does not eliminate them.

Before you decide to write a will and do nothing else for estate planning, make sure you consider two factors: (1) the total value

---

- Personal property, real estate, and stocks and bonds
- Checking and savings accounts
- Community property
- Businesses
- Life insurance proceeds from policies on the estate owner and life insurance policies on others owned by the estate owner
- Interests in trusts established for the estate owner by others
- Vested retirement benefits

FIGURE 10.1 Examples of Assets That Could Be Included in Wills

of all your individual assets, or what they might be worth when you die, especially if they include real estate in an area of growing popularity or growth stocks, and (2) the drawbacks of the probate process.

1. **Total estate value**—When you consider your house(s), bank accounts, stocks and bonds, tangible property, and life insurance, you will probably reach the current $675,000 allowance for Unified Tax Credit (UTC) more quickly than you thought you would. The UTC allowance is the amount the surviving spouse can leave to children and other heirs tax-free. (See Figure 10.2 for UTC allowance increases through 2006.) When the total estate value reaches $1,350,000, professional estate planning with a lawyer who specializes in the field is crucial. There are ways, some of which are discussed in this chapter, to take advantage of both spouses' UTC allowances, leaving $1,350,000 to heirs tax-free.

2. **Probate process**—Other factors often overlooked are the three drawbacks of probate law: delay, cost, and lack of privacy. The probate process takes a minimum of nine months and often two to three years, even with a relatively simple, uncontested estate. Probate costs, such as legal, accounting, and executor's fees and court costs, can total 3% to 5% of the total estate. This can amount to $50,000 or even more, for a $1 million estate. Finally, all records are public. Anyone with the inclination to visit city hall, or even go online to the Internet, can peruse the details of who inherited how much and what.

The IRS is increasing the UTC allowance on this phased basis:

2000: $675,000
2002: $700,000
2004: $850,000
2005: $950,000
2006: $1 million

FIGURE 10.2 Programmed UTC Allowance Increases

Estate Planning: The Basics

For these reasons, a basic estate plan contains more than just a simple will and should start with a **revocable living trust.** This is an instrument that enables you to organize your estate and facilitate its quick passage to your heirs when you die. It is called a living trust because an estate lawyer prepares it while you are alive, and the fact that it is revocable means that you, the trust creator, can add and remove assets as your personal financial situation changes. Once you set up a trust you will transfer most of your assets—stocks, bonds, mutual fund shares, other investments, real estate—to it and you will serve as trustee.

The three most important advantages of a living trust are privacy, avoidance of probate, and creation of a framework for estate tax planning, as shown in Figure 10.3. Another potential advantage is asset protection. In certain situations, a trust can protect the assets it contains from the creditors of a beneficiary, or from a spouse or former spouse if the beneficiary goes through a divorce. (Trusts are not, however, a substitute for prenuptial agreements. If you are concerned about protection of wealth as you enter marriage, you need

	Leaving all property to spouse	Funding family trust with exemption equivalent
Total assets	$2,000,000	$2,000,000
Marital deduction	($2,000,000)	($1,000,000)
Amount to family trust	—	$1,000,000
Federal estate tax due on 1st spouse's death	—	—
Taxable estate of surviving spouse	$2,000,000	$1,000,000
Federal estate tax due at death of surviving spouse (after credit)	$435,000	—

This example is based on the $1 million UTC allowance that will come into effect in 2006. As this book goes to press in 2000, the UTC allowance is $675,000.

FIGURE 10.3 Effect of a Properly Funded Trust on Estate Taxes

a lawyer who specializes in this field.) The trust can also provide for special needs of a beneficiary, related to education, health, or physical or mental capacity.

Lastly, a living trust provides the framework for tax planning, helping couples take full advantage of the UTC allowance for both spouses while assuring the surviving spouse of sufficient asset availability for his or her comfort and security.

In conjunction with a revocable living trust, you should develop and execute a **pour-over will.** This type of will is typically used to bequeath only tangible property, such as jewelry, artwork, or tools. The remaining property, which can include securities, money-market funds, and real estate, will then pour over into the revocable living trust.

In addition to an updated pour-over will and revocable living trust, the basics of sound estate planning include a **living will, power of attorney for health,** and **durable power of attorney for property.** The forms and stipulations of living wills and powers of attorney for health vary from state to state and require the assistance of a lawyer who is licensed to practice where the client lives. Nonetheless, their basic function is uniform from one jurisdiction to the next.

A living will has no effect on property, but entrusts life-and-death decision-making authority to someone you appoint should you become terminally ill, fall into a coma, or otherwise be incapacitated to the point where you cannot speak for yourself. Typically, but not necessarily, people designate their spouse, children, or siblings to make these decisions.

A power of attorney for health instructs doctors and other health care givers whom to deal with if you are incapacitated. The person entrusted with this authority signs release forms for surgery, gives authorization to administer drugs, and makes all the decisions that you would make for yourself, if you were able.

A durable power of attorney for property empowers an agent (again, typically a close family member) with broad authority to make business and financial decisions. The word durable means that it will remain in force if you are incapacitated. The agent, or attorney-in-fact, can write checks, pay bills, prepare tax returns, and make retirement elections. Given to someone who is trusted completely, this instrument can be extremely useful if you are incapacitated.

Gifts Versus Bequests

In many cases, intelligent estate planning calls for your avoiding inheritance tax by giving assets to future heirs while you are still alive. You may be aware of the so-called $10,000 tax-free gift allowance but think that it is not very significant. Wrong! Consider the provision that you can give $10,000 each to as many recipients as you want. A good example of maximizing this allowance is a married couple with two married daughters, each of whom has two children—a total of eight future heirs (two daughters, two sons-in-law, and four grandchildren). The couple can give $20,000 ($10,000 from the husband and $10,000 from the wife) to each of those eight people for total tax-free giving of $160,000. And, they can do it every year. If they can afford it, they can give their heirs $800,000 in five years, tax-free.

□ □ □

Gordon and Iris Little, Inc.

The Littles were an excellent example of people who underestimated the amount of their estate and the complexities of structuring it to benefit those they favored. Gordon graduated from the U.S. Naval Academy in 1960, served three shipboard tours in the coastal waters of Vietnam, and retired as a captain in the mid-1990s. His military pension and frugal savings habits provided amply for himself and Iris, whom he'd met at an Annapolis mixer and married right after graduation.

They retired to a cottage on five coastal acres in Maryland that provided Iris with the flower and vegetable garden she had missed during 38 years of frequent relocation, the fate of a military wife. It was also close enough to Annapolis for Gordon to attend alumni events, which he enjoyed immensely. Early in retirement, Gordon, physically fit and still vigorous, bought a dilapidated, 46-foot yacht and refurbished it himself, mooring it at a nearby marina. The restoration took the better part of two years, but provided a sailboat that was as beautiful and valuable as it was fun to navigate.

Quite intelligently, the Littles relied on Gordon's pension for fixed income and invested their savings in blue-chip stocks and U.S. Treasurys. They also maintained modest savings accounts for quick access to a few thousand dollars should their grown son, who was married, responsible, and supporting his own family, encounter an unexpected extraordinary need. At their first meeting with us, the Financial Physical (Appendix A) made two things clear: (1) Their finances were in sound shape and their portfolio did not need drastic reallocation. (2) The Littles were in urgent need of estate planning, drawing on the expertise of more than one specialist.

Their estate, including real estate, savings, the yacht, and family heirlooms, totaled more than $1.5 million, "quite a bit, for an old sailor," as Gordon observed at that first meeting. We made two immediate recommendations: Involve their CPA for tax expertise and an estate lawyer for inheritance law knowledge. They should also involve their son, Bruce so he would understand his projected inheritance and plan his own estate to care for his wife and two children.

At first, Bruce resisted. He said that his parents owed him nothing and that he did not want to think about their death. Eventually, we and his parents were able to persuade him to understand that, by not participating in the planning, he was depriving himself of important information. Gordon's common sense finally prevailed with Bruce. Gordon pointed out that planning for his and Iris' death would not precipitate the event, but merely prepare everyone for the unavoidable.

Acting as the COO of the Littles' virtual company, we coördinated the Littles, their son, the accountant, and the lawyer. The lawyer prepared a living trust; Gordon and Iris recognized its advantages over their prior arrangement, a will. Over several months, Gordon and Iris worked with us to structure a gifting strategy. Leaving the bulk of their estate to Bruce, they also provided gifts for nieces and nephews. Especially rewarding to Gordon was a significant bequest to a Naval Academy fund for children of the class members of 1960 who were killed in the line of duty. They also provided gifts for their local church, county hospital, and, at Iris' insistence, the Society for the Prevention of Cruelty to Animals (SPCA).

Finally, we scheduled a meeting with Gordon, Iris, Bruce, the lawyer, and the accountant to review all the decisions and documents. Gordon and Iris expressed happiness and satisfaction, along with the resolution to read the documents one last time and sign them.

Less than two weeks later, our secretary said Iris was on the line. We took the call eagerly, assuming she was calling to tell us she was mailing the signed papers. Instead, we heard, "Gordon died of a heart attack last night."

To compound the sadness of the sudden and unexpected death, Gordon had signed none of the trust documents. He and Iris had not changed any of the beneficiaries to include the nieces and nephews or the veterans' children's fund at Annapolis. Nor had they reregistered any of the accounts into the trust. As a result, everything passed to Iris and the estate lost the shelter of Gordon's UTC allowance, $600,000 at the time.

Still, it was not too late. Since Iris had inherited everything, we could still help her execute the trust documents as we had planned with Gordon. Unfortunately, Iris could not right herself after Gordon's death. She remained too emotionally devastated to deal with these matters. Even when Gordon was alive, she had not had the emotional wherewithal to grapple with such decisions and had always deferred to him. With him deceased, she refused even to discuss these matters with us and died shortly thereafter.

"She had no desire to live without Dad," was Bruce's explanation.

The simple will she and Gordon had drawn up prior to the discussions with us about converting to trusts was in effect. This caused the entire $1.5 million estate to pass to their son, again, without the shelter of Gordon's UTC allowance, and to enter the excruciatingly slow probate process. None of the nieces and nephews, Annapolis, the SPCA, or any of their other heirs were provided for at all. And then the situation got worse.

While Bruce's inheritance was dragging through probate, he was killed in a skiing accident. Gordon and Iris' entire estate then went to Bruce's widow, who remarried shortly thereafter. Gordon worked a lifetime serving his country, and he and Iris saved frugally. They laid careful plans for the disposition of their assets after death, favoring their son and his wife, but also providing for other relatives and charities—none of whom received a dime.

Lesson: Do not delay. You never know how long you will live. Plan, execute, fund the trusts, and sign the documents. That's the only way to ensure that your wishes are carried out.

Patrick and Irene Knight

Pat and Irene Knight planned intelligently and effectively for their retirement. Childless, they had both worked for 30 years and retired in comfort and security. Social Security, pensions, and savings·provided a comfortable life, especially since they had paid off the mortgages on their primary residence in New England and their Florida condominium.

For occasional extras, including international travel every year, they drew on their portfolio of mutual funds invested in blue-chip and large-cap stocks and in corporate bonds. Even though they considered themselves to be indulgent, in reality they withdrew less than the full appreciation in most years, and so their assets increased.

The Knights were long-time clients of ours, and at each annual review for many years, we uncovered no need for asset reallocation; they were living in comfort as their portfolio grew every year. However, they had no estate plan, just a simple will leaving everything to each other. They told us that they wanted to benefit certain relatives and charities, but that whichever one survived would do that once he or she probated the will and ensured his or her own security.

At every annual financial review, we counseled establishing an estate plan. We pointed out that the Knights could provide for the survivor and also determine who and what would benefit when the second one died. But following our recommendation would have required them to contemplate each other's death and the ensuing loneliness. Neither wanted to leave the other alone, nor be left alone and, as a result, the counsel went unheeded. Then nature and fate intervened.

Nature struck in the form of a sleet storm one February morning, and fate placed the Knights in an intersection as a dump truck skidded through a stop sign. Their weekly excursion to their favorite grocery store, as much a social experience as a commercial one, landed Pat and Irene in the intensive care ward. Elderly and frail, they could not recover from their head and internal injuries. Irene died that day and Pat followed before week's end.

Since they had each left the entire estate to the other and had no children, state law dictated disposition of their estate. It's safe to assume that they had desires about who would inherit what, but state law has no way to account for the unexpressed desires of the deceased.

If Irene had wanted to leave her antique gold earrings to a favorite niece, or Pat wanted to leave his treasured shotgun to a neighbor's son, the executor knew nothing of those wishes and so could not honor them. Relatives, friends, charities, alma maters—all those whom the Knights would have benefited—lost out.

Furthermore, since they had left everything to each other, and since Irene predeceased Pat, even though by only a few days, Pat inherited the entire estate and so it all passed to his family members, with Irene's siblings receiving nothing.

Ken Yoshimura, Inc.

Half of marriages end in divorce, or so sociologists and statisticians tell us. Ken Yoshimura's story illustrates how divorce can be a complicating inheritance factor—one of many that make estate planning essential.

Ken retired at age 64 after a 42-year career as a financial analyst with a Fortune 500 corporation. He had saved throughout his career in a 401(k) plan and preceding tax-deferred savings plans and was collecting a pension and Social Security. A client of ours for several years, he formed Ken Yoshimura, Inc. as a virtual company upon his retirement, with himself as CEO and us as COO. We oversaw Ken's retirement portfolio, and his background made the semiannual asset-allocation reviews unusually spirited. Nonetheless, Ken was more than satisfied with his investment appreciation and was living quite comfortably.

Ken lived with his second wife, Julie, in a beautiful town just outside Washington, DC. His first wife lived in New England and their four grown children were raising families in four Eastern and Midwestern states.

At each annual review, we complimented Ken on his foresight and self-discipline in providing for his retirement and urged him to apply that intelligent approach to estate planning. We repeatedly posed questions such as the following:

- In what proportions do you want to benefit your first wife (who had remarried also), and second wife (who was a widow with substantial inheritance of her own)?

- Should your children from your first marriage share equally with the children of your second marriage, who were born to your second wife and her first husband?

- Do you want to benefit all grandchildren equally?

- Do you want to make one-time gifts to any family members or include them in your final bequest?

- Do you want to transfer assets to your second wife while you are still alive or only upon your death?

- Who should benefit from your life insurance? Your IRAs? Your 401(k) plan contents?

- Who should receive your valuable personal effects, including jewelry, a wristwatch, a collection of antique playing cards, and a restored 1933 Lincoln roadster?

Sober and sensible in discussions about his portfolio, Ken became irritated and impatient when we urged him to confront his own death. His wife and children were no help, because they felt it was mercenary of them to urge him to plan for them after death.

Ken died in 1998 with no estate plan, not even a will. His assets were in disarray. Conflict and turmoil resulted among relatives. Ken may have known how he wanted his estate distributed, but he failed to provide for his wishes. Probate lawyers representing various heirs and relatives are still fighting as this book goes to press. Distrust, acrimony, and multiple time zones divide family members, leaving us to shake our heads and contemplate wistfully the clarity and harmony that should have been.

Lesson: Estate planning is not a one-time task. Your family situations, business arrangements, and personal goals change. In addition, tax law is in constant flux. As a result, once you prepare a comprehensive estate plan, you should review it every three to five years.

Lessons of Chapter 10

Estate planning assures the prompt, fair distribution of assets as the bequestor intends. It minimizes taxes and maximizes family harmony, and all it requires is smart advisors and the ability to face the inevitable. You should have a familiarity with some of the essential tools of estate planning and should be able to seek estate planning counsel and service from experts, ask those experts the right questions, and understand the recommended strategies.

■ ■ ■

Professional's Toolkit

Helping a Client Prepare an Estate Plan

It can be difficult enough to persuade clients to save and plan for retirement, but at least you have one key factor in your favor: Virtually everyone likes to anticipate a peaceful, secure, relaxed retirement.

Estate planning requires an entirely different mindset, one that is considerably more difficult for many people. Here, you are asking your clients to anticipate not retirement, but death. Even more frightening is that, in many cases, you are asking a husband and wife who have spent their lives together to face the inevitability that one of them will have to survive the other, perhaps by years. Statistics tell us that most wives will outlive their husbands, who often have been the dominant financial provider. A woman's life expectancy is longer than a man's, and most men marry younger women. The thought of losing their husbands, whom they have loved and who have supported them, is too threatening for many women to face.

Although these sorts of thoughts are unpleasant and intimidating, they are extremely important. Often, clients will say to you, "We're not rich. All we need is a will." In many cases, you will find they have not realistically evaluated the total worth of their own estates. Especially with real estate appreciation, many people who do not think of themselves as rich will leave estates far in excess of the current (year 2000) $675,000 UTC allowance, the amount of an estate that is sheltered from inheritance tax.

Only a person who literally does not care what happens when he dies—to his assets or his potential heirs—can afford to die intestate, that is, without a will. Many clients will find ways to be too busy to discuss estate planning with you. We have found that with many clients, gentle, persistent reminders that ignoring these issues can cost their heirs, often adult children and young grandchildren, hundreds of thousands, or even millions, of dollars will often persuade them to start the estate planning process.

Others are more susceptible to the argument that failure to put in place an estate plan will sacrifice much of what they worked for to the government. Try asking them, "Don't you think the government has taxed you heavily enough in life? Do you want Uncle Sam to grab your children's and grandchildren's inheritances too?" Also try telling your clients that estate planning provides peace of mind, because they will know that they have done their best to provide for their loved ones. This powerful argument for estate planning is 100% true.

Appendix D, titled "Estate Planning Worksheet," offers some suggestions about how to help clients overcome their reluctance and begin the process of designing and executing an estate plan.

The Dangers and Pitfalls of the "Poor Man's Will"

A married couple who tells you they don't need a will and can avoid probate without a trust, may be relying on **joint tenancy with right of survivorship.** This allows two people to arrange to transfer assets when one dies, without probate. The problem is that joint tenancy only postpones probate, rather than eliminating it.

Let's say that a married couple places their assets in joint tenancy, and the husband dies first. His widow receives all those assets, avoiding probate. But when she dies, her estate enters probate unless she has added her children or other heirs as joint tenants on every single asset. This is a large administrative task and carries its own dangers. For example, while the widow is alive, one of the heirs could have a judgment rendered against him or her, resulting from a business failure, personal injury, or divorce. In this case, the person who brought the suit could claim a portion of the joint tenancy assets, possibly leaving the widow with insufficient funds to live.

Several Advanced Estate Planning Tools

Many of your clients will find that they benefit themselves and their heirs significantly with a more sophisticated estate plan than the basic one outlined in this chapter. If you are not an estate lawyer, you will need to involve one in this process.

This chapter's toolkit, as well as those in several following chapters, explains in detail many of the instruments an estate lawyer may recommend to clients for their estate plans.

One of the first options that an experienced estate lawyer will consider is the **bypass trust** (or **family trust**) to provide inheritance tax savings. With a bypass trust, a married couple can take advantage of both of their UTC allowances, which allow them to bequeath up to $1,350,000 ($675,000 each) tax-free. Otherwise, one allowance vanishes when the first spouse dies and passes all assets to the surviving spouse under the Unlimited Marital Deduction. The UTC allowance is increasing gradually toward a 2006 total of $1 million per person, so married couples will be able to leave estates of $2 million tax-free, if they have a bypass trust.

For example, consider a married couple with adult children and other relatives to whom they want to leave bequests. Both partners draw up bypass trusts, which they use to earmark specific assets for their children and other heirs. Let's say the husband dies first. Upon his death, his UTC allowance permits the first $675,000 of his estate to fund his bypass trust. His wife does not inherit the assets in the trust, but she is allowed to spend 100% of the income generated by those assets while she lives. In addition, depending on the trust provisions, she may be able to spend up to 5% of the principal annually, or sufficient funds from the principal to maintain her lifestyle. When she dies, the assets in her husband's trust bypass her estate and flow directly to the heirs. Therefore, the husband's allowance, which would have been lost if his wife had inherited everything, is preserved. Furthermore the wife's allowance shelters the first $675,000 of her estate from inheritance tax. The result is that a total of $1,350,000 of the couple's estate flows tax-free to their heirs.

Qualified terminable interest trusts (QTIP trusts) are designed to give married couples the ability to provide income to whichever spouse survives the other, while restricting the surviving spouse's access to the assets that generate the income. They are called "qualified" because all assets placed in a QTIP must qualify for the Unlimited Marital Deduction from taxable assets under federal estate law. "Terminable interest" means that the trust specifies who will receive the assets when both husband and wife die.

Why would a couple want to restrict the surviving spouse's access to assets? One typical reason is to ensure that their children inherit certain assets when they both die, even if the surviving spouse remarries. The QTIP trust offers the best of both worlds: The surviving spouse can live off the income of the assets protected by the deceased spouse's QTIP trust, and the children will inherit those assets when the surviving spouse dies.

QTIP trusts and the other instruments described in this chapter are extremely complex. We are only scratching the surface of these strategies. Implementing them requires expert legal counsel and service.

Irrevocable life insurance trusts (ILITs) are legal instruments that own life insurance policies and receive the proceeds from those policies when the insured person dies. Since the ILIT holds the policies outside the estate, the proceeds are not subject to federal estate tax. They are designed to enable people to provide funds to pay the taxes that will be due on their estate when they die, so their heirs will not have to come up with the money or sell part of their inheritance to pay estate taxes.

Many people do not realize that the life insurance policies they own are included in their estate and that the proceeds are subject to estate taxes, unless they pass to a spouse under the Unlimited Marital Deduction. Insurance policies owned by ILITs pay the death benefits to the trust, not to the heirs of the person who is insured, free of federal inheritance tax. The ILIT trustee then uses the proceeds to pay estate taxes, relieving the heirs of that burden. Since the trust creator pays for the insurance policy with monthly policy premiums, in effect he or she pays the estate tax with pennies on the dollar. ILITs are available in individual and joint forms. The joint form, also called last-to-die insurance, enables a married couple to provide for the inheritance taxes that will be due when they both die.

ILITs require great care and expert legal advice. For example, it is important to remember that, when you purchase an insurance policy for an ILIT, the cash value is a taxable gift to the heir who will inherit the assets. Also, a three-year rule governs insurance policies transferred into ILITs. If the insured person dies within three years of making the transfer, the proceeds of the policy are not considered outside the estate, and they are subject to federal estate taxes. Lawyers who have served our clients have most often advised to have the ILIT purchase new policies rather than having the insured person purchase the policies. This avoids the three-year rule.

Long-Term Care: Protection for the Later Years

"I've got all the money I'll ever need, if I die by four o'clock."
—*Henny Youngman*

"Money cannot buy health, but I'd settle for a diamond-studded wheelchair."
—*Dorothy Parker*

What Is Long-Term Care?

In addition to planning for the distribution of your possessions after your death, as discussed in Chapter 10, you need to think about the possibility that you may not be able to care for yourself in the final years of your life. As difficult as this type of planning is for many people, it is essential. Without financial provisions for long-term care, you risk the following heartbreaking scenario:

1. Working, saving, and investing for a lifetime to fund a secure, comfortable retirement;

2. Planning to benefit your heirs after death; and then

3. Dissipating all your money in the last few years of your life and seeing your work and planning go to naught.

Long-term care is the support you may need when you can no longer care for yourself. Long-term care insurance provides coverage for the day-to-day expenses you might incur for support and assistance if serious illness, accident, or disability leaves you physically or cognitively unable (or both) to care for yourself for a long period.

Long-term care is provided in a variety of settings: a nursing home, nursing facility, assisted living facility, alternate care facility, or your own home. Long-term care coverage is purchased by individuals and couples for themselves and for aging parents and other relatives. Its appeal is its ability to shelter the assets accumulated over a lifetime that you may want to leave to heirs, charities, or alma maters. While no one wants to contemplate years in a nursing home, consider two statistics. (1) The U.S. Senate Select Committee on Aging estimates that our population over age 85 will be seven times its present size in 50 years. (2) *The New England Journal of Medicine* reports that, of those who live to age 65, one in four will spend at least one year in a nursing home and one in eleven will spend at least five years there.

As life expectancy increases, many Americans will enjoy retirements of 20 to 30 years. But those longer life spans will also inflict a variety of chronic illnesses or disabilities on many elderly Americans. More than five million Americans need some type of long-term care, which they receive at nursing homes or in their own homes, from relatives or paid caregivers. Yet, almost half the people over age 85 need help with everyday, basic tasks, such as eating, dressing, or going to a doctor.

There is much confusion about what Medicare and Medicaid cover. Medicare pays for skilled nursing care for a limited period of time, if the patient meets strict requirements. This nursing and rehabilitative care must be performed by skilled medical specialists, and it does not include the ordinary custodial care that many older Americans require. Medicaid is only available to persons who have depleted their financial resources to a level of poverty. So, without private provision for long-term care, many seniors are trapped in the Medicare-Medicaid gap. They are too wealthy to qualify for Medicaid, and find that the care they need is not provided by Medicare. This is why it is essential that you confront, plan for, and finance long-term care.

Evaluating Long-Term Care Options

What would you do if you required long-term care? Would a spouse or family member take care of you at your own home? Would you move into the home of a family member? If your family required assistance with your care, where would they obtain it? And how would you pay for it? Would you be forced to liquidate IRAs and investment accounts?

If you decide your situation requires the need to plan for long-term care, you should consider these factors:

- **Age**—The younger you are when you buy the policy, the lower the annual premiums will be. The longer you wait to purchase the policy, the higher the premiums. If you purchase long-term care at age 50, versus age 75, you will pay a lower premium for a longer period of time. Even though a 50-year-old may pay the annual premium for 25 years, the total outlay will be far less than a 75-year-old paying for 10 or 15 years.

- **Health**—Annual premiums for the same coverage will vary depending upon your health. Medical conditions can and will increase the cost of the policy depending upon the severity of your personal condition.

- **Coverage**—Annual premiums vary depending upon the type and length of coverage you select. Will you settle for only nursing home care? Home health care? A combination? More complete coverage costs more.

- **Length of coverage**—Will you need coverage for three years, five years, or for life? The longer the duration, the higher the annual premium.

- **Deductible**—Are you willing to pay the first 30, 60, or 90 days in the nursing home or home health care out of your own pocket? A longer waiting period means a lower annual premium.

- **Daily benefit**—This is the amount your policy will pay per day either for nursing home care or home health care. In addition, you need to be aware of the services that are included with your coverage.

- **Inflation option**—Inflation takes its toll on everything including long-term care. The cost of the policy is affected by whether you choose a simple inflation rate or a compounding inflation rate option. If you are in your 50s, this is a more important feature to consider than if you are in your late 70s.

- **Marital status**—Many carriers offer a spousal discount for long-term care policies. Inquire about this.

- **The company**—Since this could be a long-term relationship with the company you select, it should be a solid, highly-rated, and reliable company. Nationally, there are probably 100 or more companies that offer long-term care.

□ □ □

Wilbur and Alice Morgan, Inc.

Wilbur and Alice Morgan were the quintessential salt-of-the-earth couple. Married after high school, they saved their hard-earned pennies to put a down payment on a tiny Cape Cod-style house in a semi-rural town in Rhode Island. Wilbur worked as a printing press operator at a large manufacturing company, where Alice was the switchboard operator. With the arrival of twin daughters, Alice happily left the company to care for and raise the girls—a responsibility the Morgans deemed much more valuable than the wages Alice had been earning.

With annual increases from the company that appreciated loyalty and longevity in its employees, Wilbur's salary was ample to afford the family of four a modest lifestyle. Alice, a talented seamstress with a knack for making beautiful creations out of remnants, always made sure the girls were dressed stylishly. She diligently bargain-hunted for used furniture and home accessories and made the little house a warm family home. There was always an inviting aroma from the old crockpot that sat simmering on the kitchen counter, waiting for Wilbur and the girls and any of their friends who might drop in.

As the girls approached college age, the Morgans knew that they would need to rely on aid from scholarships and loans to send the girls, both of whom had great academic aspirations, to the colleges of their choice. Admissions letters brought welcome news. Both daughters were accepted with full scholarships to Boston University—one to the School of Education and the other to the School of Nursing.

Throughout college, the girls supplemented the meager weekly allowance that Wilbur was able to provide with on-campus jobs.

They returned home during each vacation exhausted from the strain of studying and working. The stress paid off, however, as both girls graduated cum laude and quickly found jobs in their fields of interest.

As printing technology was advancing, the company where Wilbur worked was slowly updating the equipment Wilbur used to produce forms and flyers. Because he was such a devoted, long-term employee, the company agreed to sell Wilbur the used equipment well below market value. Wilbur set up the old presses in an unheated shed he and his brother constructed in the yard and, with the company's blessing, took on side jobs.

We first met Wilbur and Alice three years ago. They dropped in at their neighbors' house with freshly baked oatmeal raisin cookies, just as we happened to be conducting an annual review meeting with the neighbors, who were long-time clients. Embarrassed that they had interrupted the meeting, the Morgans deposited the cookies and left. The next week, however, we received a call from Wilbur, who said that meeting us had finally given him the impetus he needed to focus on managing and preserving his retirement assets.

Wilbur, age 69, had amassed a portfolio of $480,000 in his 401(k) plan, which had been rolled over into an IRA at his retirement seven years before. He and Alice were both healthy and lived simply and comfortably with funds from his pension, Social Security, and modest income from the small print jobs he still took on. Their Financial Physical revealed that they wanted to provide a substantial inheritance to their daughters so that their grandchildren would not have to work their way through college the way their daughters had.

We reorganized the portfolio within various private asset money managers, according to MPT, described in Chapter 4.

Then Alice voiced a concern. Her mother had lived out the final three years of her life in a nursing home, and the cost of that care had used all the money she had ever saved, leaving Alice nothing upon her mother's death. She didn't want that to happen to her own daughters.

We told the Morgans about the benefits of a long-term care insurance policy, which would accomplish exactly what Alice wanted. Although it was difficult for Alice and Wilbur to contemplate such a possibility, they discussed it and agreed that purchasing a policy would be prudent. The policy cost $4,800 per year, or about 1% of their total portfolio.

About six months after the policy went into effect, Wilbur called to tell us that Alice had suffered a severe stroke that had paralyzed her entire right side and left her unable to perform most of the activities required for daily living. She would be leaving the hospital within a few days, and he needed nursing assistance at home. We assured him that the policy they had purchased would take care of the cost of this home health care.

Over the next 10 months, Alice lived with round-the-clock nursing care in the little house she and Wilbur had bought more than 50 years before. Both daughters were married with children of their own and lived several hours away. They visited often to care for their mother. Disappointingly, Alice showed little promise of improvement and ultimately suffered a series of mini-strokes that eventually took her life.

Without the long-term care coverage, Wilbur gladly would have spent the $50,000 it cost to provide the care required for his loving wife. But the policy performed exactly as designed. Although Wilbur is devastated by the loss of his lifelong partner, he appreciates the fact that, as he and Alice wished, their children and grandchildren should benefit from the preservation of their assets.

Lessons of Chapter 11

Many of you, either firsthand or through friends, have endured the emotional toll and financial burden of caring for a loved one either in a nursing home or in a home health care setting. By anticipating and prefunding this type of care for your own elder years, you can ensure that you won't burden your family with these costs, nor will you deplete the inheritance you intend for them or other beneficiaries.

■ ■ ■

Professional's Toolkit

Helping Clients Understand Long-Term Care

If your clients aren't sure if long-term care insurance is appropriate for them, these three hypothetical examples may help.

- Consider a couple in their late 50s contemplating retirement in a few years. They have an investment portfolio of $2.5 to $3 million. In addition, their combined pension will be $8,000 to $10,000 per month, and both will qualify for Social Security. In this scenario, they are unlikely candidates for long-term care insurance. They could use either pension or income from investments to self-fund long-term care at home or in a nice facility. If needed, they could also liquidate a portion of the investment portfolio. Their income and portfolio should be able to bridge the cost of any care that is not covered by their medical insurance.

- Now consider a retired couple in their early 60s with an investment portfolio of $300,000 to $500,000. They also have a home that is paid in full and a small condo in another part of the country. If the need arose, the cost of a nursing home could total $4,000 to $6,000 per month, per person. Pension and Social Security for both spouses is in the range of $4,000 per month and, when one spouse dies, this will be substantially less. Paying for a nursing home or home health care out of their own pocket could dissipate their investment portfolio. A nursing home facility or home care could total $8,000 to $12,000 per month if needed for both spouses at the same time, totaling $96,000 to $144,000 per year. Under these circumstances, a long-term care policy covering both spouses is a better solution than having their income and investment portfolio depleted.

- The final scenario concerns a retired couple with pension and Social Security of $2,500 per month. They have lifetime savings and investments of $100,000. The idea of purchasing long-term coverage is certainly appealing, however they cannot afford the annual premium. In such a case, your client will need the advice of a lawyer who specializes in Medicare-Medicaid planning.

Spend It:
The Ultimate Family Vacation

"Almost any man knows how to earn money,
but not one in a million knows how to spend it."
—Henry David Thoreau

A Happy Dilemma

At last, a chapter about the fun part—spending, rather than accumulating, money. What good is money? It is as good, or as bad, as the uses to which you put it.

The suggestion that a financial professional might have to advise you on how to spend money may seem absurd, but we have encountered this need repeatedly with clients. People spend their whole lives saving, investing, and living frugally to avoid dependence in their old age. Then when they reach their elder years with assets that assure their independence and security, they often have trouble adjusting to a new way of thinking. In short, they have to be coaxed into relaxing and enjoying the financial security for which they have labored for decades.

So, suppose you have the funds you will need to maintain your lifestyle as long as you live and to obtain medical care you may need in your declining years. You have provided for those people and institutions you care about after your death. What do you do now? Relax and enjoy the rest of your life.

□ □ □

Dr. and Mrs. Henry Bradstreet, Inc.

A pediatrician, Henry Bradstreet established an extremely successful medical practice, where he worked 40 to 50 hours per week and
drew a salary of $100,000 per year. Although he loved caring for
children, Henry realized in his late 50s that, at some point, he would
not be able to work 50-hour weeks and provide the uncompromis-
ing quality of patient care that he demanded of himself. He decided
that he could provide for his patients and position himself for retirement by bringing a young doctor into his practice.

Much to his delight, his nephew, Alex, became that young doctor. Henry and his brother, the young man's father, had been close
throughout childhood and into their adult years—best friends, as
well as brothers. As a result, Henry loved his nephew, who was his
brother's only child, almost as much as his own children. He would
often refer to Alex as his fourth son.

So when Alex followed Henry into the medical profession, even
attending the same medical school, Henry was proud and satisfied
and secretly hoped they might practice together one day. When his
nephew chose pediatrics as his specialty, Henry was elated and
made his nephew the following offer:

"Join me in my practice, and at the start we will divide the income two-thirds to me and one-third to you. As you establish yourself, earn board certification, and win the patients' trust, we will
gradually increase your responsibilities and your income so that,
within a defined period, we will be dividing the patient load and the
income 50–50. As I reduce my patient load, with total retirement as
the ultimate goal, we will gradually increase your share of the income. When I retire, you will take over the practice as your own,
with no capital investment, and pay me a fixed stipend for life that
you and I will decide on at the time."

Henry and Alex agreed that they would rely on their accountant,
who specialized in working with small professional-service firms,
for advice on the exact schedule of shifting the patient load and the
income. They also fixed a timetable for Alex to earn pediatric board
certification and secure a teaching appointment at any one of several medical schools in the area. In addition to the business, financial, and medical goals and schedules, there was also a bond of love
and trust between them that gave both men the confidence they

would not have irreconcilable differences. That confidence was borne out over time.

Henry was able to make this generous offer because he and his wife, Diane, had lived a modest lifestyle. They had saved about $550,000 and paid off the mortgage on their $100,000 home. They did allow themselves some luxuries, such as eating supper in restaurants weekly and vacationing at a resort in Puerto Rico for two weeks every winter. They also gave money to their sons, all three of whom were married and raising families of their own. But the Bradstreets certainly were not lavish or ostentatious in their spending, nor had they burdened themselves with credit card or other kinds of silly debt.

They had also helped their three sons by providing much of the capital to buy a plastics injection-molding and zinc diecasting business that was failing, but that the sons thought had potential. The sons were right in that assessment, but turning the company around required an 11-year investment of sweat equity by all three. Nonetheless, by 1999, their diligence had paid off. The company was registering more than $10 million in annual sales, employed several dozen people, provided income for the sons, and was worth on the open market many times what they and their father had invested in it. Seeing their three boys working together, building a business they owned, gave the Bradstreets almost as much satisfaction as if the three had become pediatricians and joined their father and cousin.

It was Diane who urged Henry, at age 64, to consult a financial advisor. From talking with friends their age, Diane sensed that she and Henry could benefit from expert financial counsel and a plan for the rest of their lives. Although the couple felt wealthy because of their close, loving family, Henry revealed a dream that surprised even Diane—to make himself a millionaire. He and Diane came from working-class families and had put themselves through college, and Henry through medical school. It was not for greed, but for a desire to affirm his self-made success that Henry sought the $1 million.

When the Bradstreets first met with us in 1989 after attending one of our seminars, they told us they wanted to structure their portfolio for growth. Yet, the Financial Physical revealed that virtually all of the Bradstreets' $550,000 was invested in bond funds. The bank had handled everything. "What did we know about investing?" Diane asked. "Nothing."

Considering their goal of asset appreciation, this made no sense to us. Henry was still working full-time in his medical practice, and his agreement with his nephew guaranteed him and Diane a fixed income even when he reduced his workload and eventually retired. Taking these factors into account, we recommended a total shift to equities. The Bradstreets agreed. Together we structured their portfolio based on the MPT principles discussed in Chapter 4, designed to provide long-term growth. We brought an estate planning attorney on board who drew up and executed revocable living trusts, durable powers of attorney, living wills, health care proxies, and simple wills. We then made sure the trusts were funded properly. The Bradstreets said, "We don't need this money now. It's for a God-forbid event or emergency financial needs."

The Bradstreets implemented their new strategy rigorously. They adopted a sensible, long-term view of their investments, resisting the temptation to jump in and out. In short order, they reached Henry's $1 million goal and raced past it. Their original $550,000 portfolio totals $2.5 million as this book goes to press in 2000. This is an almost overwhelming amount of money to the Bradstreets, who remain unassuming, down-to-earth people. At age 70½, the law forced them to begin to take distributions that they did not want from their IRAs. By 1999, those withdrawals totaled $90,000 to $100,000 per year. The Bradstreets asked us, "What are we supposed to do with all this money?"

In 1999, the Bradstreets put the final piece in place, prepaying their funerals and other burial expenses. They did not need long-term care insurance because their $2.5 million portfolio was more than sufficient for any possible future needs of this type. Henry and Diane both suffer health problems that prevent them from prepaying their sons' inheritance taxes with life insurance trusts. As a result, they have more money than they ever dreamed and limited options in sheltering it from estate taxes. They literally cannot spend the money they have, in spite of repeated entreaties from us to travel, fly first-class, stay in luxurious resorts, and buy new cars.

Their sons and daughters-in-law join us as the COO of Dr. and Mrs. Henry Bradstreet, Inc. in urging their parents to spend money.

They say that, largely thanks to Henry and Diane's parental and financial support, they are self-sufficient.

"We don't need your money and we don't want it," they say. "Listen to your advisor and spend it on yourselves."

The Bradstreets' family—their sons; daughters-in-law; five grandchildren; and nephew, Alex and his wife and children—remains the center of their lives. Both Henry and Diane can give $10,000 per year to each of their loved ones without paying gift tax or having the recipients incur income tax. This totals a potential annual tax-free gift of more than a quarter-million dollars. In strong market years, they take advantage of this gifting option to some extent.

To solve the happy dilemma of having more than sufficient funds, we sat down with the Bradstreets and asked, "If you could do anything in the world, what would it be?"

"Have a family vacation on a sunny beach," they said, after some thought and discussion. Henry and Diane polled their sons and daughters-in-law, and their nephew and his wife about the best spot for a family vacation, compliments of the grandparents. St. Thomas won. They selected luxury resort suites for the six families, inviting Henry's brother and his wife as well, overlooking the ocean.

They were contemplating horseback riding, wind surfing, golf, tennis, sailing, snorkeling, and four-star dining when we said, "That's not good enough." At our insistence, they upgraded from the resort to a rented villa, staffed by servants and offering access to the facilities of local hotels and a private club. It proved to be the family vacation of a lifetime and, even better, the Bradstreets can afford to do it every year. The entire family agreed that they would all take two weeks a year for similar vacations as long as mom and dad wanted and were able to do so. They have achieved true wealth.

Lessons of Chapter 12

Once you have achieved your financial goals, change your mindset to enjoy the financial security you have reached. It will admittedly be difficult suddenly to shift focus from saving to spending, but take pride in your accomplishment. Have the security and the confidence to live the lifestyle you envisioned, the one that motivated you to work hard, plan, and save for so many years.

■ ■ ■

Professional's Toolkit

What's Important to Your Clients?

We hope this chapter has provided a vivid picture of one family's definition of wealth: old-age security for mom and dad, leavened by the ultimate annual family vacation. To some people, two weeks on a beach would be an exercise in boredom and futility. They'd rather build Habitat for Humanity homes in Africa, plumb the Jurassic depths of Western Europe, or disappear into the timeless maw of Las Vegas.

How can your clients identify what is important to them in life, and can you help them do so? Too often, we have to lose someone, some gift, or some capability to realize the answer to this question, or even to ask it. In a miserable cell of the Hanoi Hilton, undergoing daily torture, Senator John McCain learned what is important. Katie Couric learned at the deathwatch for her husband. Christopher Reeve learns it every day as he copes with an accident that took an instant but endures for years.

Some of us are luckier. Death threatens someone dear to us, but, at the last minute, steps back and, for unfathomable reasons, spares us. Or we are moved by a loss suffered by a friend. Radio talk-show host Don Imus has established a ranch for children with life-threatening diseases, having been inspired by the example of Hamilton Jordan and the death by sudden infant death syndrome (SIDS) of a colleague's baby.

Matt Dawson, who appeared on Oprah Winfrey's television program in the fall of 1999, decided the most important thing to him was to give underprivileged youths the college education he never had. A forklift truck driver, Dawson was still working double shifts at age 79 to endow scholarships. For 25 years, he donated 50% of his salary, determined to give $1 million to this cause.

We would be a more advanced species indeed if, like Dawson and like the Bradstreets, most of us could fix on a goal, undistracted by the desire for that next promotion, raise, bonus, or uptick in the stock market.

How can you help your clients, not to mention yourself, in this regard? From your first meeting with a client, when you should review the Financial Physical (Appendix A), you should probe to find out what is important to them. Is it security, luxury, charity, independence? Is it providing for progeny or caring for elderly parents? Is it a vacation in Europe or summer house on the beach?

The first challenge is to ask the right questions. The second is to establish the kind of client relationship that will enable and encourage them to answer. Third is to define your role in the discussion. Is it financial advisor or more? Friend, psychologist, confidant?

Understanding the client's total financial situation and financial and lifestyle goals is the minimum. How much more you become to your clients is up to you.

CHAPTER

Leaving a Legacy—Wisely

"Money, which represents the prose of life, and which is
hardly spoken of in parlors without an apology, is,
in its effects and laws, as beautiful as roses."
—Ralph Waldo Emerson

The Importance of Intergenerational Communication

Imagine that you are the adult child of a father who founded and
has operated for 50 years a company that manufactures flower pots.
You never had even a glimmer of interest in working in your father's flower pot business. You have become a well-respected antiques dealer, having pursued your childhood dream by serving ap-
prenticeships and receiving advanced education within your chosen
field. One day, shortly after your father dies, his lawyer calls you
with the news that your father has left the flower pot business to
you, with the stipulation that you oversee the entire operation while
you simultaneously continue your career as an antiques dealer.

The lawyer tells you, "Your father's wish was that the business
stay in the family. He worked his whole life to make this business
what it is today, and he wanted to make sure that you didn't just liquidate it and possibly squander the proceeds. He wanted you to make
sure it continues operating successfully in the spirit of its history, so
that someday your children can have the opportunity to run it."

You are speechless. You have no idea of the scope of the operation, nor the plans he had envisioned for the company, let alone how
to run it successfully.

While this is a seemingly far-fetched scenario, it is fairly analo-
gous to what happens within many families when the parents die

and leave the execution of a sizeable estate to an unprepared child or children. The children, most often adults themselves, are usually unfamiliar with the estate plan their parents had put in place, and many times are completely unaware that their parents had amassed such a significant amount of assets over their lifetime. In many cases, these beneficiaries have little, if any, experience or training for managing the distribution of the estate among family members and are ill-equipped to preserve their share.

Now imagine a similar situation to the one described at the outset of the chapter, but instead of leaving you with the sole responsibility of running the business, your father, in his later years, prepared you for the transition. He told you of his intention to leave you the business and introduced you to his senior staff, who would be working for you to continue to operate the business successfully. He shared with you important information about the business, helped you bone up on the flower pot industry, communicated to you his future plans for the business, and familiarized you with the staff who would be implementing the plans. He encouraged you to continue your work in the antiques field, while simultaneously overseeing the managers whom he had trusted with the business during his living years.

Under this set of circumstances, you would probably feel much more secure when your father passed on, since you would already have established a relationship with the company's managers, and you would not be left on your own to handle the operation. The same is true for beneficiaries. Depending on your current stage in life, you should be apprised of your parents' estate plan, bring your children into your own estate planning process, or both. How can you be reasonably sure that your beneficiaries carry out your wishes for the set of assets you have worked so hard to amass? The key to effective transfer of wealth is communication. Involve your heirs in the planning process. Take the opportunity to tell them what they stand to inherit, how you earned it, what you intend for it, and how you made those decisions. Make sure they understand the responsibility that comes with managing an inheritance. Prepare them for that responsibility.

In addition, introduce your children to your estate lawyer and financial planner, or meet those with whom your parents have been working, since those professionals will essentially be implementing the estate plan. This will give your children the opportunity to develop a relationship with the financial and legal professionals with whom they will be working, so they can feel confident that they are not left alone to manage the tremendous responsibility. Although we are conditioned to believe that it is not polite to discuss finances, it is important to give your children a sense of the amount they stand to inherit and begin to give them a fundamental understanding of how they can manage it for preservation. Too many children are stunned by the amount left to them by their parents, whom they had assumed were worth far less due to the frugal lifestyle they had embraced.

Helping Your Heirs Understand Financial Concepts

In the best case, you are leaving an estate to children or other family members who have developed prudent earning, saving, and spending habits. These people understand the value of money and will respect the time and energy you expended to earn the assets in your estate. You can be confident that your heirs will strive to preserve your largesse without a notion of frivolity. But this is not always the case. Quite possibly, you are leaving your estate to heirs who are not especially savvy regarding finances, investments, and preservation of capital. One of the best gifts you can give to these heirs during your living years, is a fundamental understanding of these concepts. And if you rely on your financial advisor to help you understand these concepts, it makes perfect sense to include your heirs in this education process.

Of course, the optimal course of learning about finances occurs over a lifetime, and ideally you should begin to introduce money management concepts to your children when they are young. This goes a long way in building a sense of responsibility and instilling healthy and prudent financial habits. As young as age four or five, you should talk to your children about money. You don't need to discuss how much money you earn. Your objective should be simply to introduce your child to three basic ideas: (1) that you earn money by working; (2) that you use money to pay for things your family needs, such as food, clothing, the house, and the car; and (3) that you save and invest money to meet larger goals like a family vacation or higher education.

It is important to remember that kids learn by example. For instance, you teach your kids to brush their teeth, and you set a consistent example by brushing your own teeth every day. Following your lead, your kids will brush their teeth, even though they don't understand the concepts of tooth decay, cavities, and gum disease. The same holds true for money management. Your kids need to see you exercising a consistent approach toward money management; they don't need to understand about interest rates, the stock market, or economic cycles.

You can teach the most basic lesson about saving even to a toddler by beginning with a piggy bank. With an older child, parents can set up a bank account for their child and explain how money grows just by sitting in the bank. You may even want to match the deposits your child makes into his or her account. Both of these exercises instill the habit of setting aside money for future needs.

Giving children an allowance is another good way to teach financial responsibility. Many parents expect their children to do common household chores to earn their allowance. This teaches kids that money is a limited resource, a lesson best learned at a young age.

As your children reach the age of 9 or 10, begin discussing the concepts of investing in stocks and bonds. Select companies recognized by children, such as McDonald's or Gap, and track their performance in the newspaper. When the children get older, buy individual stocks or mutual funds to give them a feeling of ownership in the company.

One of our clients invested an unexpected inheritance in several mutual funds for her 10-year-old grandson. She showed the young boy the funds' prospectuses, and out of his own interest, he read them. Now when they shop together, he constantly reminds her which products and services they should be buying based on the names of the companies he recognizes from his mutual funds!

Another client started even earlier. She purchased 18 shares of Walt Disney Company stock for each of her four children as soon as they were born. She framed each stock certificate and hung it on the wall in the stockholder's bedroom. She and her husband want their children to grow up familiar with the concept of investing.

You can introduce older children to the myriad books and Websites that teach money management skills and concepts exclusively to kids. As they begin to earn money from a summer job or other employment, help them open up an IRA. This will get them into the habit of saving early for their retirement, something you may wish you had done at their age.

Communication Can Help Reduce Estate Taxes

All this discussion about the need to educate your children about your estate and its ultimate disbursement is underscored by the fact that upwards of $41 trillion will be passed intergenerationally over the next 50 years, according to the Social Welfare Research Institute at Boston College. Candid intergenerational dialogue can help families set up their estates to reduce tax liability. For example, open communication between parents and their adult daughter may reveal that the daughter is very well established financially. Inheriting her parents' entire estate outright would cause the estate to be depleted with taxes upon inheritance. The proceeds would then be added to the daughter's own estate, which would be taxed again upon her death. The multiple taxation would result in a significant deterioration of the original inheritance to future generations.

In this case, the parents might consider creating a long-term dynastic trust. By funding such a trust with their generation-skipping transfer-tax exemption, the parents would be able to give their daughter the use and control of the trust and its assets, but at the same time exempt the trust assets from estate taxes when the daughter dies, when her children die, and probably when her grandchildren die as well. In some states, such as Rhode Island, where there is no legal limitation on the duration of trusts, estate taxes for successive generations can be completely eliminated through the dynastic style trust. Because the trust is estate tax-exempt regardless of growth, the family has the power to exponentially grow the trust for future generations to use as a family bank forever! Of course each family's situation is different, and you need to consult an experienced estate planning attorney to determine what might be appropriate for your family's situation. The point is, however, that without involving multiple generations in the estate planning process, it is impossible to identify the circumstances that might needlessly deplete an estate.

☐ ☐ ☐

The Donaldson Family, Inc.

We met Joe Donaldson in 1989 when we presented a retirement seminar at the steel plant he worked for in Pittsburgh. In his late-50s at the time, Joe was the human resources manager at the company. After we finished our talk to the 60 or so plant workers in attendance, Joe approached us and said we had hit a nerve. He was looking toward retirement in about five years, and had a lot of questions about how he should prepare. He also told us that his wife was particularly anxious and uneasy about their financial future. We suggested that he set up a meeting with us the following day and encouraged him to bring along his wife.

The next afternoon, Joe and his wife Margie arrived for our meeting carrying a pile of meticulously kept financial records. As we had advised, the Donaldsons had completed in detail the Financial Physical (Appendix A) and brought with them recent account statements. Margie, who looked to be a year or two younger than her husband, admitted that while she did an admirable job of keeping the family's financial records, she had little knowledge of what they meant. She had deferred to Joe over the course of their 36-year marriage in making decisions involving financial matters, but while she knew he had done a prudent job of managing money relying on his steady income, she was unsure that they had saved enough to last throughout a long retirement.

Looking over the records, we determined that the Donaldsons had amassed about $1 million, scattered among a wide variety of mutual funds and CDs. Our discussion with them revealed that they lived fairly modestly in the home they had purchased shortly after they got married, which had quadrupled in value over the years to be worth about $120,000. They always wanted to keep $100,000 liquid, making them comfortable that they had a little over one year's spending money plus an extra cushion for emergency expenditures. A review of their estate showed that, while they had created and executed simple wills, they had not developed an estate plan to preserve assets for their two daughters, Cheryl and Stephanie, who were each married and raising children of their own.

The Donaldsons told us they wanted to make sure they had enough assets at retirement to have $100,000 income annually.

They had calculated that this amount would enable them to live comfortably without having to work, while affording them the ability to travel several times a year. We estimated that their portfolio would need to grow to about $2.5 million for them to make reasonable withdrawals of 4 percent, or $100,000 per year. In addition, the Donaldsons sought to structure their portfolio in such a way as to minimize estate tax liability for their daughters when they inherited the estate.

Our first step was to focus the Donaldson's investments. Using MPT, we divided the funds among several private money managers and focused Joe's 401(k) portfolio in three stock funds: a blue-chip fund, a mid-cap fund, and an international fund. As the Donaldsons requested, we kept $100,000 in T-bills and a money-market fund for liquidity. Secondly, we introduced the Donaldsons to an estate planning attorney and helped Joe and Margie put in place the recommended estate documents, including a revocable trust, pourover wills, durable powers of attorney, and living wills.

We met with the Donaldsons twice a year to review performance and update their financial plan according to changes in their situation. By the time Joe retired five years later, the portfolio had grown to just over the $2 million mark. We rolled over Joe's 401(k) into an IRA and the Donaldsons continued their commitment to the investment plan. As it has turned out, the Donaldsons had overestimated the amount they would withdraw from their portfolio annually during their retirement years and actually spend about $50,000 each year to fund the activities they wish to do. This has resulted in a portfolio that is worth $5 million today.

Realizing that this sizeable estate would be subject to heavy taxation upon both deaths, last year we recommended that the Donaldsons update their estate plan. At our meetings over the years, Joe and Margie had talked proudly about the achievements of their daughters and, even more so, about their four grandchildren. They had always emphasized the importance of education in their family and anticipated great academic achievements from their grandchildren. Considering this focus on education and knowing the need to redo the estate plan, we suggested to Joe and Margie that they consider creating a dynasty trust. This would enable them to leave a large portion of their estate to be used for their grandchildren's educational needs, as well as possibly the needs of their great-grandchildren. They were thrilled with the idea and consulted an estate attorney, who properly structured the trust. We also encouraged the Donaldsons to spend more money from their portfolio. This sparked in Joe and Margie the idea of giving annual monetary gifts to their daughters, so they could see their hard-earned money put to good use while they were both alive.

With their new estate plan in place, the Donaldsons decided that they should apprise their daughters and sons-in-law of the arrangements they had made. They asked us to help them educate their children about the plan and how it works, and included us in their family meeting. We helped Joe and Margie explain to Cheryl and Stephanie and their husbands about the estate plan they had put in place. Joe and Margie outlined the rationale behind the plan, as well as their wishes and desires for the use of the money for education within the family. We educated their children about the purpose of the trust and how it functions, as well as the importance of preserving the assets. The first reaction of the children was that they were flattered but wanted their parents to spend more money on themselves. Joe and Margie explained that they were not holding back in their spending, that they were, in fact, fulfilling all their dreams. Cheryl and Stephanie thanked their parents and made it clear that the future inheritance would not change their current values. They realized the importance of working, earning income, saving diligently, and spending wisely.

At the end of the meeting, we all expressed our hope that we wouldn't see the tax benefits of the trust for many, many years. But when the estate does indeed pass down, the Donaldsons' children will understand and appreciate the forethought and generosity of their parents.

The Worthington Family, Inc.

Doug and Naomi Worthington have been our clients for six years. Doug is the Chief Information Officer at a well-known consumer products manufacturer. Naomi, a former fashion model, has spent the past 26 years in the most noble profession—as full-time mother to the couple's two children. In their late-40s when they came to us, the Worthingtons sought our help to establish a growth portfolio and to strategically allocate Doug's 401(k) assets. With an original portfolio worth $1 million, the Worthingtons now have amassed almost $3 million.

But that's not the most interesting part of the story. While we certainly have been impressed over the years with the Worthingtons' ability to save and adhere to the financial plan we developed, what has struck us more is their desire to instill in their children the values and good money management habits they possess themselves. Kate and Garrett Worthington have always been the subjects of praise by their parents at each annual portfolio review and during almost every telephone call. When we began working with their parents, Kate was finishing her second year of undergraduate studies at Johns Hopkins University and Garrett had just been accepted into the freshman class at Cornell.

The academic accomplishments of each child were truly worthy of their parents' acclaim, and we were not surprised to hear two years later that Kate was graduating from Johns Hopkins with honors and had been accepted to Brown University Medical School. As an extremely generous graduation gift, Doug and Naomi set up an account with us for Kate containing $10,000, which she would be responsible for overseeing. The Worthingtons instructed their daughter to work with us to invest the money as a way to foster practical education and encourage her to build a relationship with us. They restricted her from spending it.

A neophyte investor, Kate took her newly bestowed responsibility seriously. She wanted to learn about the stock market, and we decided to invest the money in companies Kate would be interested in following. As a nod to Kate's future medical career, we bought shares of Pfizer. As Kate was an avid runner, we invested in Nike. And to round out the portfolio, we decided that Kate should own some Gap stock, as she told us she was a lifelong customer.

Similarly, two years later, when Garrett graduated at the top of his class at Cornell, Doug and Naomi granted their son the same opportunity for financial education, funding his account, as well, with $10,000. As we got to know Garrett, we learned that, like his father, he was deeply interested in systems technology, and he also was skilled at home building and repair. We suggested that he make his initial investments in Microsoft, Intel, and Home Depot.

With both young investors, we talked in detail about the companies in which they were buying shares. We discussed earnings, historical stock performance, corporate growth opportunities, and industry sectors. We taught Kate and Garrett the basics of portfolio allocation, and they have learned firsthand about the factors that impact market cycles. They have each called us with ideas for investment opportunities; some we pursue, and others we dismiss with a solid explanation of why it is not prudent for their portfolio. In every monthly statement of their accounts and every conversation with Kate and Garrett there lies a lesson about the importance of saving and investing wisely.

Some children may have seen the $10,000 as a gift in itself; both of the Worthington children see it for the twofold gift that their parents intended. While they are grateful for their parents' monetary generosity, they embrace even more the opportunity to learn about investing and preserving their own wealth.

Lessons of Chapter 13

In many cases, inherited wealth is more difficult than earned wealth to keep intact and manage. Take the opportunity to educate your heirs, no matter what their age, about the importance of saving and investing. Communicate openly about your estate plan with your heirs so they can prepare to wisely preserve it.

■ ■ ■

Professional's Toolkit

Initiating Legacy Planning with Clients

Legacy planning is a highly sensitive but critical part of providing financial counsel. Many clients do not want to face their own mortality and are uncomfortable discussing personal financial details with their children. You can provide an invaluable service by guiding them through the estate planning process and by helping to demystify the complex concepts that are integral.

Many people take a reactive, rather than proactive, approach to legacy planning. They often initiate the process during emotionally troubled times, making the planning even more painful. You can help them avoid this by beginning the dialogue with them, using their life events as a springboard for the conversation. Listen to what is going on in your clients' lives. An unexpected inheritance, an illness, a financial milestone, or a birthday close to retirement age are all good starting points for you to introduce the subject.

As you have developed a financial plan specifically for each client, you should develop a legacy plan to meet each client's needs. Focus on your client's goals and concerns, and consider all the components of your client's financial picture. Be willing to educate the heirs about the plan, and encourage your clients to communicate openly with their heirs about their plans. Remember that a good legacy plan not only benefits the inheritors financially, it also can reduce the burden of many issues they will face upon wealth-transfer.

Give It Away:
For Those With
Strong Charitable Motivation

"The highest use of capital is not to make more money,
but to make money do more for the betterment of life."

—Henry Ford

"If you give money, spend yourself with it."

—Henry David Thoreau

The Desire to Benefit Others

Statistically, Americans are the most generous people in the world.
We see those statistics brought to life by client after client. Most of
our clients' definitions of wealth include the ability to benefit
someone or some organization—family, friends, alma maters, or
charitable institutions—when they die. Yet, this is also the most
commonly overlooked aspect of financial planning by people who
are reasonably organized and foresighted about their family goals.
It is also an area where expert counsel is vital.

Estate and inheritance law is complex and ever changing. Of all
the sections of this book, this is as likely as any to change significantly in the months between completion of the writing and publication. Unless you are a tax lawyer who keeps current on the latest
changes, this is an area where you, as the CEO of your virtual company, and your COO will need to involve a specialist.

Here are two Wealth Stories of generous women. Neither earned high incomes in life, but both achieved wealth. In both cases, wealth was largely defined by what they could do for others.

□ □ □

Helga van Leewen, Inc.

More people fantasize about wealth than plan and save for it. What would you do with an unexpected windfall of a quarter-million dollars? Helga van Leewen lived that fantasy and, although a retired widow of modest means, she gave away $250,000 that she had earned and saved, but that she refused to regard as her own.

Born in 1919 in Erie County, Pennsylvania, not far inland from the Lake, Helga graduated from high school—the first in her family to do so—in 1937 and married her high school boyfriend. Helga took a job as a clerk in the engineering department of Atlas Aircraft Company, a local manufacturer of private, single-engine and twin-engine airplanes. Within a couple of years, she and her husband saved enough money for a down payment on a modest house and began what they expected to be a long life together, raising a family. Then, World War II intervened and left Helga a young widow by 1944. She never remarried and kept working in the aircraft company engineering department.

During the ensuing decades, Helga paid off the house and proved herself a frugal saver. Following the example of her engineer-colleagues, she took advantage of all payroll-deduction and savings plans her progressive employer offered.

"I figured the engineers were smarter than I was," Helga said, "so when they signed up for a savings plan, so did I." When the engineers authorized payroll deductions for war bonds, so did she. When the engineers participated in an employee stock option plan, so did she. When the company was acquired by a conglomerate based in New York City and established a 401(k) savings plan and the engineers signed up, so did Helga.

Helga retired with 45 years' service in 1989. The aircraft company's Human Resources Department could not explain her assets and financial options clearly, so, once again, she asked her engineer friends what to do. Several of them were our clients, so Helga followed their lead.

When Helga came to the first meeting with us, she was wealthy, by her own modest definition. She had paid off the house that she and her husband had moved into in 1939, and received about $12,000 annually from her pension and $8,500 per year in Social Security. Through various savings plans, she had accumulated about $25,000 in the aircraft company's stock and $15,000 in mutual funds and bonds. Dividends and interest on this $40,000 paid her about $2,500 per year. In total, she received almost $2,000 per month, which was about 85% of her annual salary in her final working years. Childless, she was generous with her nieces and nephews, traveled internationally every year, and still saved money.

As the prescribed first step in providing financial counsel, we reviewed all Helga's assets and made a happy discovery. In addition to what we have described above, Helga had almost $250,000 in a 401(k) plan that she did not realize she had! Financial reports can be difficult for professionals to decipher and impenetrable to lay people. This was the case with the reports that Atlas Aircraft Company and its corporate parent provided to employees.

"It's not my money," was Helga's initial, shocked reaction. She could not sleep for a week. She was determined: "This is God's money, not mine. I must give it away."

We explained that she had worked for and earned the funds, that they were part of her compensation for 45 years of diligent, loyal service. But Helga would not be dissuaded. So we set about helping her identify an appropriate charity to benefit from her generosity. Helga told us that, never having had children of her own, she wanted to help others' kids, especially babies. In addition, she had yearned for higher education as a youth, but her father thought that was not appropriate for women; as a result, she ended her formal education with her high school diploma. Therefore, she wanted to help the nurses who cared for infants with their education.

With this charitable objective, she formed Helga van Leewen, Inc. and appointed us COO.

We determined that, if Helga simply withdrew her $250,000 in the tax-deferred savings and paid the taxes, she would be able to donate substantially less than $150,000 to charity. Working with a local CPA whom Helga trusted, we determined that the best course was to establish an irrevocable insurance trust with a not-for-profit organization as beneficiary. We then reinvested the $250,000 from the 401(k) plan into a qualified annuity that would generate $15,000 annual payments into the insurance trust and an additional small annual sum to Helga that we hoped she would spend. If Helga lived just 10 years, the hospital would receive about $500,000 when she died—more than three times as much as if she'd simply donated the 401(k) plan savings.

The next step was to identify a worthy charity to benefit from Helga's generosity. We recommended several alternatives, and Helga selected a nearby, university-affiliated hospital that specialized in obstetrics and gynecology, the health and medical care of women and their babies. The CEO and COO of Helga van Leewen, Inc. toured the hospital and met with the senior doctors and administrators. Helga was especially engaged by a neonatal unit that cared for premature babies.

Helga established the St. Christopher's Fund at the hospital, naming it for the small community hospital in her hometown where she and her brothers and sisters had been born. The fund's mission was to provide financial aid to nurses pursuing bachelor's or master's degrees, or professional training. It was also constituted to fund research into neonatal therapies and care. As the irrevocable trust accumulated funds for a major bequest after her death, Helga made periodic small donations, including presents for children and gift baskets for the caregivers, whom she referred to as "my nurses." In 1989, we had reinvested the $40,000, the original sum she thought she had when she first came to us, in blue-chip, dividend-paying common stocks and growth-oriented mutual funds. With this strategy, the $40,000 plus a little money she still managed to save, grew to $100,000 between 1989 and 1994. At that point, we shifted the funds to a global stock portfolio run by private money managers. The money managers selected U.S. and European Union blue-chip stocks, concentrated in utilities, food, pharmaceuticals, and telecommunications companies, building the $100,000 to $185,000 by the end of 1998.

The appreciation of her portfolio coupled with her prudent budgeting, enabled Helga to travel throughout Europe, Africa, Asia, and North America, including Alaska, and still donate about $5,000 per year to charity for the second half of the 1990s. She made frequent trips to the hospital with no fanfare, visiting the neonatal care unit, hospitalized children, or the nurses—never the executive suite.

As we write this book, Helga has just died, almost exactly 10 years from the creation of the annuity and insurance trust, having added her house to the hospital's bequest. As a result, the hospital is receiving approximately $750,000 from their benefactor who never earned as much as $30,000 per year, but who formed a virtual company in order to provide for babies and help nurses in perpetuity. In her view, this was the most appropriate use of "God's money."

Louise Upton, Inc.

The dictionary tells us that the word "frugal" (thrifty) is derived from the ancient Latin *frugalis*. Privately, we suspect the word was invented to describe our client Louise Upton.

Louise, a retired librarian, lives in a University town in the Corn Belt of the Midwest. We met her more than 10 years ago at an afternoon retirement-planning seminar we delivered near her home. She approached us as everyone was leaving and we were cleaning up the refreshments, complimenting us on the talk and asking, "Are you going to do anything with those leftover cookies?" When we offered, she gladly accepted them. That was the start of a relationship that led to our appointment as COO of Louise Upton, Inc.

Had we known Louise since her childhood, we would have expected her inquiry about the leftover snacks. As a child, shortly after the turn of the century, her father would take Louise and her sisters to the agricultural fairs that are prevalent in the Midwest. He would give each daughter a dime, enough in the days before World War I for an ice cream cone and a ride on the carousel. Her sisters would spend their dimes gleefully, but Louise always saved hers, even when her father urged her to indulge just five cents for an ice cream.

When we met Louise in 1988, she was in her early 70s and had retired as the librarian in the town where she had grown up and attended teachers' college. She still lived in the house her father and uncle had built, was driving a 20-year-old rattletrap, mowing her own lawn, setting her own hair, and volunteering at a local seniors center to help "the old folks."

After sizing us up at several sessions of our seminar, Louise scheduled a meeting. She had started buying mutual funds in 1951 and had accumulated about $900,000 in stocks, bonds, mutual funds, CDs, a bank savings account, and a tax-sheltered annuity. Her frugality was admirable; accumulating nearly $1 million on the salary of a town librarian demonstrates an amazing ability to save. But her portfolio had no focus and no direction.

In addition to her $900,000 in savings, she had a public-employee pension of $15,000 per year and Social Security payments of $5,000 per year, plus income from a boarder in her home. Never married, she was focused, like Helga van Leewen, on having her savings benefit others after she died. Her goal was to leave $1 million after taxes to her relatives and a substantial bequest to her alma mater and the local library where she had spent her career. As she appointed us COO of Louise Upton, Inc., we advised her that $400,000 of her $1 million estate would be subject to estate taxes. At the time, the unified credit allowance was $600,000.

Our first steps as COO were to do the following:

1. Organize and consolidate the investments into blue-chip, dividend-paying equities and fixed-income securities

2. Fund an irrevocable insurance trust with $50,000 per year for 10 to 12 years from her portfolio. This would provide $1 million tax-free to her heirs. Louise liked this idea because she felt that if something happened to her when she was "still young," she could still provide the sum she wished to both the nieces and nephews and her beloved charities.

3. Prepare estate documents, leaving $1 million tax-free to her nieces and nephews and $300,000 divided equally between the library where she has worked and her alma mater.

From 1989 to 1999, as we write this book, she has increased her portfolio by $300,000 via new savings from part-time jobs and investment appreciation. Frankly, we cannot figure out how she saves this amount of money on her income. She has been and remains the single most self-disciplined and successful saver we have ever met—including ourselves.

We have persuaded her to upgrade from a dangerously dilapidated twenty-year-old car to a safe, five-year-old used car. She still has her 1950s chrome-and-Formica kitchen furniture and appliances. As this book goes to press, Louise is in her early 80s. She no longer has her boarder, but we still cannot get her to hire a neighborhood teenager to mow her lawn. We have, however, gotten her to buy a used, self-propelled mower.

Louise has her health, has provided for those people and institutions dear to her, and certainly has wealth by her definition.

Lessons of Chapter 14

The most important principle of this chapter is that most people who accumulate any substantial amount of money—and we don't mean only the super-rich—can arrange to bequeath more money than they realize.

Scrimping and saving for decades, combined with intelligent, planned investing, can amass a substantial bequest. However, a knowledgeable financial advisor can help leverage savings. An experienced professional who understands trusts and taxes and who will involve the right lawyers and accountants can help navigate the complex inheritance and estate laws. Using the proper financial and legal instruments helps ensure that the heirs inherit what the CEO worked for, rather than surrendering an unnecessarily large portion to Uncle Sam.

■ ■ ■

Professional's Toolkit

An Advanced Estate Planning Instrument: The CRT

The charitable remainder trust is a vehicle that you and the tax lawyer may want to consider, especially during strong stock-market periods. If investors' assets have appreciated significantly, the charitable remainder trust provides income to the investors while they are alive and enables them to benefit nonprofit organizations when they die.

The charitable remainder trust converts highly appreciated assets, including stocks, bonds, and real estate, into a lifetime income stream for the owner, avoiding capital gains taxes when he or she sells them and inheritance taxes later, and passes the funds to a designated charity upon his or her death. It can reduce your client's income tax while the client is alive and reduce the estate taxes paid by the heirs by more than half.

When investors establish a charitable remainder trust, they arrange to receive income from the trust for a term of up to 20 years, or for life. They can also arrange for the income to flow to a spouse or other family member. Investors take several actions and receive several benefits. Specifically, they:

- irrevocably transfer assets, including cash, securities, or property, into the trust. This lowers the taxable value of their estates, providing significant estate tax savings to their heirs.

- receive an immediate charitable income tax deduction, based on their ages and the ages of the designated income beneficiaries, the distribution rate chosen, and the value of the assets transferred to the trust.

- pay no capital gains tax on assets sold after their transfer into the trust.

- benefit the charities they select when the trust is terminated. That occurs at the end of the term or, in the case of lifetime income, the death of the trustee or designated income beneficiary. They can change those charities at any point but cannot retrieve the funds for themselves or any person or organization that is not recognized by the IRS as a charitable institution.

Pitfall 7:
Force Your Heirs to Sell
Family Treasures

"Put not your trust in money, but put your money in trust."
—Oliver Wendell Holmes

"Money often costs too much."
—Ralph Waldo Emerson

Putting Family Heirlooms at Risk

Your family summer home, your family farm, your family business, or even your family's valuable stamp collection may be assets you expect to remain in your family for many future generations. But if you don't plan accordingly, the next generation could encounter a situation that is sad—even tragic—but all too common.

By now, you may realize the point of this chapter: Inadequate estate planning can force your heirs to sell precious family property or heirlooms to pay the estate taxes those inheritances incur.

It is not difficult to understand why many intelligent, educated people overlook this danger. We have seen it time and again. Consider, for example, a married couple who are third generation farmers or ranchers, working land their grandparents bought for a song 75 years ago. It is more than even a home and career combined to them; it is a way of life. The land and the passion for it pass from one generation to the next. But as this occurs, residential tracts, industrial parks, or tourist attractions grow up around it. The value of the land skyrockets, but it does not produce more cash or a higher standard of living than it did in the 1940s. In fact, it seems to the couple that they have a tougher time making ends meet than their parents or grandparents did. When one spouse dies, no estate tax problems result. The farm or ranch passes to the surviving spouse tax-free under the unlimited marital deduction.

It's when the second spouse dies that Uncle Sam appears, tax bill in hand, demanding to be paid. His state counterpart is right behind him. Although the land yields a modest living, it may be appraised, for tax purposes, at hundreds of thousands or even millions of dollars. This value produces an estate tax burden in the tens of thousands or hundreds of thousands of dollars. It does not matter that generations of the family poured their labor and their love into the land. It does not matter that every generation worked to pass the land to the next. It does not matter that the children passed up other opportunities to take over the family farm or ranch. All that matters is that there are taxes due. Where are the children, struggling to support themselves and their families from the farm income, going to get the cash? They aren't. They lose the homestead and the way of life that they love and were counting on being able to bequeath to their children.

We have seen the same ruthless principle play out with family-owned manufacturing businesses and retail shops. It can also happen with treasured, highly valued heirlooms: jewelry, artwork, coin and stamp collections, rare books, and other collectibles. More common is real estate, especially summer homes.

Maybe you and your spouse bought a summer cottage near the beach, lake, or mountains in a relatively undeveloped area years ago. You have special childhood memories of the area, having spent time there as a youth with your parents and grandparents. When you bought the cottage, you imagined your children and grandchildren sharing similar pleasures with you, and carrying on the tradition after your death. Over the decades the natural attractions in the area drew people, and land values shot upward. Suddenly, in your 60s, you discover that your children will have to sell the vacation home to pay the estate taxes on it. Here again, heritage, family, and dreams mean nothing to the tax man. All the government cares about is the money it has decided your survivors owe.

Not all of these cases are solvable with even the most expert estate planning, but many are. Happily, Henrietta and Oswald Stone fell in the latter category.

□ □ □

Oswald and Henrietta Stone, Inc.

The year was 1988 and Oswald Stone was 63 when he began to think seriously about retirement. His wife of nearly 40 years, Henrietta, was 61. Fortunately, while the Stones had not been planning for retirement, they had been saving for it. A convincing salesman and highly capable manager, Oswald had risen to the Director of Sales position in a large operating unit of a Fortune 500 corporation. Along the way, he consistently made the maximum contribution to his 401(k) plan, whose funds were invested 75% in company stock and 25% in equity mutual funds within the program.

Henrietta had been a stay-at-home mother while the couple's four children were growing up and had been occupying her time with volunteer work at a local hospital and a food bank since the youngest had left home for college.

Oswald's rise through the corporate bureaucracy had occasioned several moves, which the family willingly endured because his success made him a good provider. Another factor that helped the family endure the moves was a summer beach home on Cape Cod. No matter where the family lived during the school year, Henrietta would take the kids to the Cape Cod house for two months each summer. Oswald would join them for two weeks' vacation and on weekends.

The years of having and raising the family quickly became decades and, somewhat to their own surprise, the Stones found themselves at a retirement and estate planning seminar we presented along with a colleague who is an estate lawyer. At the conclusion of the seminar, the Stones approached us and confessed that they had considered retirement a luxury, and had not given it significant thought, despite their age. How could they afford medical care in retirement? Could they travel? Could they leave money to their children? These sorts of questions had occurred to them during the presentation.

During the seminar, the lawyer had provided an overview of many of the estate instruments and documents described in previous chapters of this book, including the simple will, living will, pour-over will, living revocable trust, healthcare proxy, and durable power of attorney. He had also discussed probate and how to avoid it, along with estate tax laws in effect. For our part, we had discussed our approach to client service, including the formation of virtual companies with the client as the CEO who appoints a COO. We also covered the importance of goal-setting, and of submitting, without embarrassment, to a thorough Financial Physical, as outlined in Appendix A.

At seminars such as the one attended by the Stones, someone in the audience invariably asks, "What stock do you recommend? Which mutual fund is hot? What is your tip of the day?"

Our response is always the same and always disappointing to many in the audience: "We cannot provide a blanket recommendation in a public setting. We cannot provide advice without knowing who you are, what your goals and circumstances are, and what your investment experience has been." Our tip of the day is consistent, day in and day out: Consider the benefits of trust accounts, estate planning, pre-retirement and retirement planning, determining a retirement budget, plotting retirement goals, creating a wish list, and creating a financial roadmap. That is the way to your retirement dreams, not trying to outguess the market or chase the latest rumor.

After a short discussion following the seminar, the Stones said they understood the benefits of running their retirement like a business, with their own specific plan aimed at specific goals. Guided by the seminar presentations, they promised to consider the five-step retirement planning process outlined that day:

1. Identify realistic financial, personal, lifestyle goals.
2. Identify constraints: time horizon, income needs, realistic rates of return, risk tolerance.
3. Understand and consider the risk/reward relationship, balancing equities versus debt instruments in a way that is comfortable.
4. Create an investment portfolio of mutual funds, stocks, bonds, and other instruments.
5. Monitor and evaluate the real rate of return with your financial advisor, relative to appropriate benchmarks.

The Stones called us about one month later to request an appointment. In our first meeting, they told us that one of their most precious assets was the summer home on Cape Cod that they visited annually. They had bought it early in their marriage for a small fraction of its current value. They planned to spend May through September at the home every year and looked forward to long visits from guests, especially their children, who had moved to different parts of the country. They were also counting on leaving the summer house to their children, who could not afford a comparable property at current prices. In addition, Henrietta had become devoted to the hospital and food bank where she volunteered. They wanted to leave money to both, as well as to Purdue University, Oswald's alma mater.

What would all this cost? Were they pipe dreams or realistic goals? The Stones had no idea.

The Stones brought their Financial Physical (Appendix A), completed in laborious detail, to our first meeting. They had included spending habits, anticipated retirement expenses, travel expenses, home remodeling expenses, pension income, 401(k) rollover account values, and IRA values. The seminar and the exercise of completing the Financial Physical led them to realize that their estate, a major portion of which was their Cape Cod home, would incur a substantial estate tax liability. For the first time, it dawned on them that their children might have to sell the home to pay estate taxes, losing a precious inheritance they would be unable to replace at current prices.

The Stones' investment portfolio was valued at approximately $350,000. Their Cape Cod home was valued in the $850,000 to $1 million range and their main residence west of Boston in the $350,000 to $400,000 range. They also had a few small insurance policies. Would it be practical, they asked, to sell their main residence and relocate to Cape Cod year-round? They would use the cash proceeds from the sale of the Boston house to pay off all remaining mortgages on the summer house and to remodel and winterize it. They knew they could take advantage of the **one-time exclusion** provision of tax law in the sale of their Boston house. If they made that improvement to the Cape Cod home, would it drive up its value to the point where the children would have to sell it to pay estate taxes? If the property appreciated as much as they hoped, just meeting the property tax bill would be an issue for their children.

In 1988, the **one-time exclusion** allowed people 55 years and older to sell a house that had been their primary residence for three of the previous five years, with no capital gains tax. Since 1998, the law has permitted a tax-free capital gain of $250,000 for single people and $500,000 for married couples on the sale of their principal residence. The requirement now is that the home was the principal residence for two of the preceding five years. Furthermore, this exemption is available every two years for an unlimited number of times.

The Stones said that their previous stockbroker, whom they liked a great deal, had never suggested an estate review or plan and had never recommended consultation with a trust lawyer. His self-defined role was to recommend and then execute purchases and sales of stocks. The Financial Physical, they said, had been an eye-opening experience for them.

People often overlook the value of their house in compiling their assets. Although real estate is a far less liquid asset than a stock or a bond, it is an asset. A complete understanding of your situation, required for intelligent financial planning, requires the inclusion of real estate as currently valued among your assets.

Review and analysis of the Stones' Financial Physical determined that Oswald's pension and Social Security would sustain their standard of living for a short time. But they would have to withdraw from the IRA and 401(k) accounts to fund entertainment at the Cape Cod home, to travel, and to offset inflation.

After this initial meeting, the Stones appointed us COO of their virtual company.

Step two was arranging a consultation with a trust lawyer to estimate estate tax liability and review the appropriate legal instruments and techniques. The Financial Physical was just as helpful to the trust lawyer in determining the size and tax liability of the Stones' estate as it was to us in asset allocation. With the estate valued and taxes estimated, the lawyer forecasted administrative, accounting, and legal expenses, as well as funeral, burial, and associated costs.

Happily, in the Stones' case, personal and family debts were not a big factor, but that certainly is not always the case.

Step three was to have an estate plan drafted by the lawyer. Since the Stones had an estate tax liability in the neighborhood of $250,000, the lawyer recommended an irrevocable insurance trust (discussed in detail in Chapter 10's Professional's Toolkit). This was the best way to ensure that the children would not have to sell the Cape Cod home to pay estate taxes and provide for estate liquidity.

With draft documents reviewed by the CEO and the COO, all that remained was to underwrite the insurance trust and complete the trust documents. At this point, we could shift focus to the management of the investment portfolio.

The Stones needed to draw on their investments primarily to provide the annual premiums for the insurance trust. We worked with the Stones to decide on a portfolio that was concentrated in equities. An important factor is that Oswald had a substantial pension and Social Security, and also had income from a marketing consulting practice he operated out of a home office. This totaled an annual fixed income of nearly $100,000, eliminating the need to structure their portfolio to provide fixed income.

The goal was sufficient annual growth to pay the insurance trust premiums and, ideally, growth above that to fund a family gifting plan. In bull market years, there would be family gifts, their size determined by the bulls' strength. When the bears ruled, the Stones would dispense with family gifts until better times.

As this book goes to press, almost 10 years have passed since the formation of Oswald and Henrietta Stone, Inc. The Stones' retirement years have been happy. Oswald and Henrietta are both healthy and have given tens of thousands of dollars to family members and various charities. The value of their portfolio has been growing and has allowed them to live the life for which they saved. Oswald is still consulting, and as he says, "I never intend to give it up. It gets me out of the house and keeps my mind active." We have also convinced the Stones to purchase long-term care insurance with some of Oswald's extra income.

Even with aggressive and generous gift giving, the current value of their account is higher than it was 10 years ago. The Stones say it is impossible to put a price on the joy of giving money to their family and charities. On our recommendation, they have revisited their comprehensive financial plan, including a consideration of the effects of continued appreciation of the Cape Cod home, secure in the knowledge that it will pass to their children. They have decided to give away as much money as they can afford to while they are alive to see its effects. They're content that, if the Cape Cod home is all their children inherit and the estate taxes are paid for, that will be more than enough. They are well satisfied. They have provided a family dream home for future generations' memories.

Lessons of Chapter 15

Many people who live in a house for a long time fail to realize its appreciation. The same principle applies to many owners of small businesses, whether they are manufacturing companies, retail shops, farms, or ranches. People work their entire lives to build a business for their children, but fail to plan for estate taxes. A summer home, farm, or ranch may be worth millions, but not produce anything close to the cash required to pay estate taxes. The heart-rending sight of a family business, family home, or family heirloom on the auction block to satisfy the government should be more than sufficient motivation to heed this chapter.

■ ■ ■

Professional's Toolkit

More Advanced Estate Planning Instruments

Following are details about two sophisticated strategies that an estate specialist may suggest for clients who want to insure the preservation of family property, heirlooms, or a family business, after their death.

- A **qualified personal residence trust (QPRT)** is an irrevocable trust that allows for a gift of one's personal residence at a discounted value for the eventual benefit of one's children. This trust may remove this asset from one's estate and ultimately reduce the potential estate taxes for the family. This sophisticated trust needs expert legal counsel to determine exactly how the trust is set up and, specifically, the length of the term of the trust. The longer the term of the trust, the more one saves on transfer taxes. However, if the individual who set up the trust dies before the term of the trust has ended, the residence will be included in his or her taxable estate, and thus the purpose of the trust will be defeated.

For individuals who have large taxable estates that include homes worth several hundreds of thousands of dollars or more, the QPRT may be an effective estate planning strategy. We recommend these individuals contact a qualified estate planning specialist for more specific details about this complex trust.

- A **family limited partnership (FLP)** is designed to reduce the value of an estate for tax purposes while allowing a person to retain use and control of the assets. FLPs are often used to pass a family-owned business from the owner/founder to the next generation, but they can also be used for other types of assets as well. Such partnerships involve general partners, who control the assets, and limited partners, who share in the profits but exercise no control.

In the case of a family-owned business, the owner/founder establishes the FLP, designating himself or herself as general partner, who runs the business, shares in the income, and receives a management fee. The members of the next generation become limited partners, sharing in the income, depending on how many shares the general partner gives them, but having virtually no say in how the business is run. When the general partner dies, the partnership is dissolved and a portion of the FLP assets pass to the limited partners, proportionate to their shares. Because the FLP shares confer no management authority and because they cannot be sold, as there is no market for them, they are appraised for tax purposes at a discounted value.

FLPs are an aggressive strategy that require expert legal assistance. You do not want your client's FLP to be the first one his or her lawyer has drawn up. Make sure you help your client obtain experienced legal counsel.

The Final Frontier

"Money is better than poverty, if only for financial reasons."
—Woody Allen

"I've been rich, and I've been poor. Rich is better."
—Anonymous

Focusing on Wealth

So you've made it to the final chapter. Maybe you've got a ways to go to accumulate your $100,000 portfolio and establish your own virtual company. Maybe you're well past that mark and on your way to $1 million. Either way, you're the one who has worked the long, arduous hours getting to where you are now, by missing dinners with the family or getting up before the sun or logging hundreds of thousands of lonely miles in business travel on cramped, impersonal airplanes.

No doubt, while enduring such thankless hours in pursuit of getting the job done, you've dreamed about what you would like to do when you have the time and funds to enjoy a more relaxed life. But just as no one has amassed your earnings for you, no one else can help you plan for that comfortable future until you take the initiative.

And while you can take the first step on your own by completing Appendices A, B, and C, once you articulate your goals, you should seek the help you need to achieve them. Don't try to do it on your own. Spend your days doing what you do best. Do it as well as you can. If you're an architect, design the best buildings you can. If you're a design engineer, devise the best products you can. If you're a salesperson, hit your quota and surpass it.

If you want to be a financial analyst, fine, be one. Earn a master's. Earn professional certification. Get licensed, and get a job at a financial services firm. Spend your working hours studying the market, devising recommendations, and tracking your results. But, if you're an architect, engineer, or salesperson, don't try to be your own investment analyst in your spare time. It's a full-time job.

Day Traders and Armchair Investors

Earlier in the book, we discussed the importance of the Internet in transforming how business does business, how shoppers shop, how schools educate, and virtually every other aspect of life. It has made detailed, sophisticated investment information and advice instantly available to anyone with a computer and a modem. Unfortunately, we believe that too many investors confuse information with knowledge and understanding

We've also talked about the temptation to try to get rich quick, investing for the short term, seeking the next Microsoft or amazon.com.

In our view, day trading is the intersection of these two bad ideas —trying to get rich quick and trying to do it yourself. It has become a craze in large part because of the publicity accorded what are supposedly vast numbers of people making fortunes overnight.

Medical doctors are licensed to practice medicine and are board certified. Lawyers are admitted to the bar. Engineers are licensed by the state. We are baffled that people who would never knowingly board a bus or an airplane operated by someone lacking the appropriate professional license will entrust their life's savings to a nameless, faceless page on the World Wide Web.

If day trading is attractive to you, read the following excerpt from an article headlined, "Heavy Losses: The Rise and Collapse of a Day Trader" from *The Wall Street Journal*, Feb. 28, 2000, p. C1:

John Nyquist traded stocks from home in the morning and hit the (golf) course after lunch. But within two years, the day-trading mother lode turned to dust. Mr. Nyquist lost all but $8,000 of the couple's $780,000 in savings, Mrs. Nyquist alleges. Then, Mrs. Nyquist says, he tried to kill her . . . Mr. Nyquist, a former chemical engineer, now is serving a five-year prison sentence in Rembert, S.C. He pleaded guilty in the fall in a Charleston, S.C., state court to a criminal charge of assault and battery with intent to kill.

In addition, on Feb. 25, 2000, *USA Today* reported that Senator Richard Durbin, D-Ill., alluded to the unsavory nature of day trading by characterizing Senate hearings into day trading as an attempt to help investors understand "what a con game is going on here."

In addition to day traders, armchair investors have slim chances of hitting it big on Wall Street. These novice investors engage in buying and selling stock based on media reports of an expert's enthusiasm. Only rarely do these broadcasted buy-and-sell recommendations pan out for the investor, because, quoting Bernard Baruch, "Something that everyone knows isn't worth knowing."

The danger in listening to a singular piece of investment advice in a media report is that the expert making the buy recommendation is not keeping you updated about the market factors affecting the stock. How will you know when that same expert thinks it's prudent to sell?

This is why you need professional investment management. You need advisors who track a broad variety of analysts regarding their projections for a certain security—whether you should buy, sell, or hold.

You, Inc.

The process described in this book for achieving wealth is tried and true. Many of our clients stand as examples of investors who have realized and seized the opportunity to insure their own financial futures, as well as those of loved ones.

There is no better time than now to give yourself the promotion to CEO of You, Inc. The sooner you empower yourself to take control of your financial destiny, the more wealth you can achieve—no matter what wealth means to you. We hope that envisioning your dreams and wishes will motivate you to make a plan for your financial future. And we wish you the best on your journey down your road to wealth.

APPENDIX

A

Your Financial Physical: Information to Take to Prospective Financial Advisors

Personal Data

Your Name _____

Spouse's Name _____

Home Address _____

_____

_____

Phone _____ Email _____

Your Business Information

    Occupation _____

    Address _____

_____

_____

    Phone _____ Email _____

Spouse's Business Information

    Occupation _____

    Address _____

_____

_____

    Phone _____ Email _____

Nationality

    You ☐ U.S. citizen ☐ Other_____

    Spouse ☐ U.S. citizen ☐ Other_____

Your DOB _____ Spouse's DOB _____

Your SS# _____ Spouse's SS# _____

Health Problems/Special Needs

You _____

Spouse _____

Please list below all living parents, children, and grandchildren of you and your spouse.

Name_____

Relationship _____ Date of Birth _____

Health Problems/Special Needs _____

Name_____

Relationship _____ Date of Birth _____

Health Problems/Special Needs _____

Name_____

Relationship _____ Date of Birth _____

Health Problems/Special Needs _____

Name_____

Relationship _____ Date of Birth _____

Health Problems/Special Needs _____

Name_____

Relationship _____ Date of Birth _____

Health Problems/Special Needs _____

Name_____

Relationship _____ Date of Birth _____

Health Problems/Special Needs _____

Name_____

    Relationship _____ Date of Birth _____

    Health Problems/Special Needs _____

Name_____

    Relationship _____ Date of Birth _____

    Health Problems/Special Needs _____

Name_____

    Relationship _____ Date of Birth _____

    Health Problems/Special Needs _____

Name_____

    Relationship _____ Date of Birth _____

    Health Problems/Special Needs _____

Marital Status

☐ Married ☐ Divorced ☐ Widowed Date _____

Please list any former marriages for you or your current spouse

_____

_____

Indicate any alimony you pay $_____ receive $_____

Indicate any child support you pay $_____ receive $_____

Estate Plan

If you have a basic estate plan, please describe briefly_____

_____

_____

_____

_____

Wills & Executor Nominations

Do you have a will? ☐ Yes ☐ No

Date of will _____ Named executor _____

Does your spouse have a will? ☐ Yes ☐ No

Date of will _____ Named executor _____

Guardian Nominations

Please list any guardians you have named for your children

_____

_____

Trusts

Do you have a living trust? ☐ Yes ☐ No

If you have any other types of trusts, please specify

_____

_____

_____

Custodianships

Have you or your spouse ever made a gift under the Uniform Gifts to Minors Act? ☐ Yes ☐ No

If yes, in what state?_____

Name of custodian _____

Names of donees_____

Trust Beneficiaries

Are you or any members of your immediate family beneficiaries of a trust?
☐ Yes ☐ No

If yes, please list who, and the expected amount

_____ $_____

_____ $_____

_____ $_____

Gifts/Inheritance

Do you or any members of your immediate family expect to receive gifts/inheritances?   ☐ Yes   ☐ No

Name of recipient _____   Amount $_____

From whom _____   When _____

Name of recipient _____   Amount $_____

From whom _____   When _____

Name of recipient _____   Amount $_____

From whom _____   When _____

Name of recipient _____   Amount $_____

From whom _____   When _____

Education

What is the level of your education?_____

Your spouse's education? _____

Consultants for Financial and Business Planning

Attorney's Name _____

    Address _____

    _____

    _____

    Phone _____

Accountant's Name _____

    Address _____

    _____

    _____

    Phone _____

Financial Objectives

Rank from 1 to 6 the importance of having adequate funds in order to do the following:

       ___ enjoy a comfortable retirement

       ___ invest and accumulate wealth

       ___ reduce federal and state income tax burden

       ___ provide college education for children

       ___ take care of family in the event of death

       ___ develop an estate distribution plan and reduce estate taxes

If you have a formal monthly budget, what is the amount? $_____

How much do you save annually? $_____

       In what form? _____

       Why?_____

How much do you think you should be able to save annually? $_____

       For what purpose? _____

How much do you invest annually? $_____

       In what form? _____

       Why? _____

How much do you think you should be able to invest annually? $_____

       For what purpose? _____

Estate Planning Objectives

Do you wish to minimize federal estate taxes? ☐ Yes ☐ No

Do you wish to utilize your (and, if appropriate, your spouse's) $600,000 federal estate tax exemption? ☐ Yes ☐ No

Would you like to avoid probate? ☐ Yes ☐ No

Would you like to learn how to pay your federal estate tax liability at a discounted rate using pennies on the dollar? ☐ Yes   ☐ No

Please list any specific estate planning objectives _____

_____

_____

_____

Factors Affecting Your Financial Plan

If you or your spouse has ever made substantial gifts to family members or to tax-exempt beneficiaries, please give details

_____

_____

What special bequests are intended, including charity?

_____

_____

Are you satisfied with your previous investment results?   ☐ Yes   ☐ No
Please explain _____

_____

_____

If there are any investments you feel committed to (for past performance, family or social reasons), please explain _____

_____

Is your spouse good at handling money?   ☐ Yes   ☐ No

In the event of your death, what is your estimate of the emotional and economic maturity of your children?

_____

_____

In the event of your death or divorce, what are your feeling about the possible remarriage of your spouse?

_____

_____

At what age would you like to retire? _____

Tax considerations aside, in what manner would you want your estate distributed?

_____

_____

What do you think your financial planning should do for you?

_____

_____

_____

_____

Investment Expectations

Investors must assume reasonable risk in order to seek increased return. Which of the following is your most important concern?

- ☐ Not keeping up with inflation.

- ☐ Short-term fluctuations that cause the value of my investment to rise and fall unpredictably.

- ☐ Loss of capital.

- ☐ Falling short of my investment-return goals.

Seeking a higher investment return generally requires accepting more frequent changes in prices and investment values. Which of the following best describes your attitude toward variability of returns—that is, swings in your portfolio value?

- ☐ My primary concern is to limit the chance of losing principal in any 12-month period. I would accept lower long-term returns in order to achieve this.

- ☐ I prefer limited variability, and I would accept below-market returns.

- ☐ I seek returns in line with market returns over an extended period and understand that temporary setbacks from market fluctuations are not uncommon.

- ☐ I am a long-term investor seeking above-average returns and I would tolerate material swings in my portfolio's value in order to pursue this.

If you began your investment program with $200,000, how large a temporary decline in portfolio value would it take to prompt you to change your investment strategy dramatically (for example, change managers, modify your asset allocation, or stop investing)?

☐ At a value of $190,000 (a %5 decline)

☐ At a value of $180,000 (a 10% decline)

☐ At a value of $170,000 (a 15% decline)

☐ At a value of $160,000 (a 20% decline)

☐ At a value of $140,000 (a 30% decline)

Investors seeking income understand that the longer the bond maturity, the greater the possible principal fluctuation. Which of the following best describes what is most important to you?

☐ My concern is maximum income and I understand that material fluctuations in bond portfolios are common with long-term bonds.

☐ I wish to have average risk associated with my bond portfolio and would prefer staggered maturities.

☐ I want minimum risk and prefer short-term bonds. I understand that yields will be lower.

Assets

This section organizes your assets. Feel free to attach a spreadsheet. Please enclose copies of all statements.

	Current Value	Specific Name/Detail
Cash		
Money-market funds	$_____	_____
CDs	$_____	_____
Cash equivalents/checking	$_____	_____
Equities		
U.S. stocks	$_____	_____
International stocks	$_____	_____
Stock options	$_____	_____

	<u>Current Value</u>	<u>Specific Name/Detail</u>
Fixed Income		
Short-term bonds	$_____	_____
Intermediate government bonds	$_____	_____
Long-term government bonds	$_____	_____
Corporate bonds	$_____	_____
Mortgage-backed securities	$_____	_____
Municipal bonds	$_____	_____
Foreign bonds	$_____	_____
EE bonds	$_____	_____
Annuities		
Fixed	$_____	_____
Variable	$_____	_____
Retirement Accounts		
IRA accounts	$_____	_____
	$_____	_____
401(k) accounts	$_____	_____
	$_____	_____
Other	$_____	_____
Mutual Funds (bonds & stocks)		
_____	$_____	_____
_____	$_____	_____
_____	$_____	_____
Life Insurance		
Your policy	$_____	_____
Spouse's policy	$_____	_____

	Current Value	Specific Name/Detail
Real Estate		
	$_____	_____
	$_____	_____
Auto		
	$_____	_____
	$_____	_____
Other		
Limited partnerships	$_____	_____
_____	$_____	_____
_____	$_____	_____
_____	$_____	_____
TOTAL	$	

Liabilities

	Amount	Interest Rate
Charge accounts	$_____	_____%
Family/personal loans	$_____	_____%
Bank loans	$_____	_____%
Mortgage	$_____	_____%
Education loans	$_____	_____%
Car loans	$_____	_____%
Other _____	$_____	_____%
_____	$_____	_____%
_____	$_____	_____%
TOTAL	$	%

Please explain any other liabilities your estate might be called upon to pay.

Clothing	$_____
Vacations	$_____
Gifts	$_____
Charities	$_____
Entertainment	$_____
Taxes—home, auto	$_____
Federal income taxes	$_____
State income taxes	$_____
Medical insurance	$_____
Education	$_____
Loan repayments	$_____
Other _____	$_____
TOTAL	**$**

Wish List

Please describe what you would like to accomplish or achieve during the rest of your lifetime, including both financial and nonfinancial goals. This will help us build the best plan for your future.

_____

_____

_____

_____

_____

_____

_____

_____

_____

_____

Questions a Prospective Financial Advisor Should Ask You

- Why are you seeking my advice?

- What are your age and marital status? Children? Grandchildren? Ages?

- What assets and debt do you have? What is your income? Do you spend more than you earn? How much do you save annually?

- Do you plan significant purchases in the near or long term?

- Do you view yourself as someone who is cautious and conservative or as a risk-taker?

- Do you have a will or trust? How recently did you update it? Have your family or financial circumstances changed substantially in the interim? May I see a copy?

- Do you have specific financial goals?

- **Most important:** What are you seeking to accomplish? What are your personal and financial goals?

Remember: The financial advisor should also ask for the information on your Financial Physical.

Questions to Ask a
Prospective Financial Advisor

When you hire a financial advisor, it is utterly different from selecting a stockbroker. Any licensed stockbroker at a reputable firm can execute the purchase and sale of securities for you. But the COO of your virtual company needs the knowledge and experience to guide your key financial decisions. The following questions are not required criteria; they are a guide to your selecting an outstanding COO for You, Inc.

- What is your education? How do you keep current with changes in the investment business?
  The person should have a master's degree in a related field—such as finance, taxation, or an MBA. They should also have achieved Chartered Financial Consultant (ChFC) status or other certifications in financial counseling, insurance, or related fields. There will be exceptions, but, in all likelihood, someone who earned a bachelor's degree in history 15 years ago and has no further degrees or accreditation, will not be the COO for you.

- How much money do you manage?
  The answer should be $100 million or more.

- What differentiates you from other financial advisors?
  If they stumble or hesitate, leave.

- What percent of your clients have been your clients for at least five years?
  The answer should be 90%+.

- What is the typical appreciation of your clients' portfolios for conservative, moderately risky, and aggressive clients?
  The answers should be, respectively, 8%–10%, 10%–12%, and 12%+.

- Will you provide me with a plan specifying, in language I can easily understand, how much of my income I can spend and must save? Will it also plot anticipated return on my investments? Will it be no more than five pages?
  You want a "yes" to all these questions.

- Do you invest in your firm's programs only or with a variety of independent money-management firms?
  You want a financial advisor who has access to programs both within his or her firm and with independent managers.

Estate Planning Worksheet

This is for financial advisors to complete with clients.

Personal Data

Name _____ Date of birth _____

Spouse _____ Date of birth _____

Home address _____

_____

_____

Phone _____ Email _____

Your Business Information

Business name _____

Address _____

_____

_____

Phone _____ Email _____

Spouse's Business Information

Business name _____

Address _____

_____

_____

Phone _____ Email _____

Current Market Value and Registrations

	wife	husband	joint
Primary residence	_____	_____	_____
Other residence	_____	_____	_____
Stocks, bonds, mutual funds	_____	_____	_____
Tax-deferred annuities	_____	_____	_____
Business property/interest	_____	_____	_____
Vehicles and boats	_____	_____	_____
Art	_____	_____	_____
Jewelry	_____	_____	_____
Heirlooms	_____	_____	_____
Other assets	_____	_____	_____
(Mortgage)	(_____)	(_____)	(_____)
(Debt)	(_____)	(_____)	(_____)
TOTALS			

■ ■ ■

Top 10 reasons your clients will give for not completing this worksheet with you:

1. I'm too young.
2. I'm not rich enough.
3. I can't decide whom to leave my money to.
4. I'll let my spouse take care of it when I die.
5. I like the will I drew up 35 years ago.
6. It's too depressing.
7. Talking about this upsets my wife (husband).
8. I'm not going to die soon.
9. It's too complicated.
10. I can't find my financial records.

Top response to all these excuses:
   "So, you want to leave the maximum portion of your estate to the government?"

Estate Planning Motivator

Posing the following questions to your clients may accomplish more than simply helping you understand their situation to provide the best advice, important though that is. The process may also help you illustrate to your clients why estate planning should be a high priority.

- Do you have a will?

- Do you have children? If so, have you selected guardians in case of your death?

- Are you entirely comfortable with those guardians?

- Are the guardians still young enough to assume that responsibility? (People often select their own parents when they are in their 20s and the parents are in their 50s. As they reach 40 and their parents reach 70, they fail to realize that their parents no longer have the health, energy, or inclination to become parents to their grandchildren.)

- Would you like to avoid probate, maintain privacy, eliminate time delays, and reduce settlement costs?

- Would you like to control assets while alive and provide for the continuing management of assets for surviving spouses and children?

- Do you realize that your biggest heir may be the IRS?

- Have you ever considered a living trust? If you have one, have you titled your assets in the name of the living trust?

- Do you want to limit your spouse's control over his or her inheritance?

- Are you familiar with the qualified terminal interest property (QTIP) provision?

- Are you taking advantage of the maximum allowed UTC?

- Is your estate more than $1.35 million as of the year 2000?

- Is a large share of your estate held in IRA, pension, or 401(k) accounts?

- Do you have an annual gifting strategy?

- Do you take advantage of the annual $10,000 gift tax exclusion?

- Have you given assets with the potential for appreciation, or might you do so?

- Have you considered the benefits of a charitable remainder trust?

- If you are self-employed, do you have a succession plan for your business?

- Is there a buy/sell agreement in place for a family-owned business?

- Have you recently purchased life insurance coverage? Who is the beneficiary?

- Do you have an irrevocable life insurance trust? If so, have you used it to exclude life insurance proceeds from being taxed in your estate?

- Is your estate plan up to date? (If the answer is, "What estate plan?" that's another way of saying, "No.")

- Are you comfortable with your estate trustee(s) and executor(s)?

Glossary

account executive Also known as a broker, investment executive, or registered representative. These financial advisors must be licensed according to product lines and states when required, and typically hold a Series 7 and Series 63 and other applicable licenses, including an insurance license.

accrued interest Interest accumulated on a bond or other fixed-income security since the last interest payment was made. At the time of a sale, the buyer of a bond pays the market price plus accrued interest to the seller. Accrued interest is calculated by multiplying the coupon rate by the number of days since the last payment.

activities of daily living (ADLs) Daily actions that people do independently, such as eating, bathing, dressing, moving about, toileting, and continence. Important to discussion on long-term care insurance.

administrator The person appointed by the court to manage an estate when someone dies without leaving a will. Having the same duties as executors, they must post a bond as security.

advisor An organization or person that gives professional advice on investments and the management of assets.

American Depository Receipt (ADR) A certificate issued by an American bank that represents a foreign stock share held on deposit. The certificate, transfer, and settlement practices for ADRs are identical to those of U.S. securities.

annuity A series of payments made or received at regular intervals or a contract that provides for a series of payments to be made or received at regular intervals. An annuity can be fixed or variable and does not necessarily have to be annuitized. It provides a means of tax deferral and in some cases provides a guaranteed death benefit.

applicable credit amount   An estate tax credit based upon the applicable exemption that reduces the tax on transfers of property either during life or at death. Created by the Taxpayer Relief Act of 1997, the applicable credit amount replaced the $192,800 unified credit with a similar credit that will gradually increase to $345,800 in 2006.

applicable exemption amount   A lifetime estate tax exemption used to calculate the applicable credit amount. The applicable exemption amount will gradually increase from $650,000 in 1999 to $1 million in 2006.

appreciation   The increase in the value of an asset.

asset   Any item of value owned by an individual or a corporation.

automatic reinvestment   A process that allows shareholders to reinvest dividends and capital-gains distributions automatically to purchase new shares.

balanced fund   A mutual fund that invests in common stocks, preferred stocks, and bonds, with an objective of balancing income and growth.

barbell portfolio strategy   A strategy by which a portfolio is weighted at each end, with short-term bonds at one end and long-term bonds at the other end with little or nothing in between. This works best when short-term interest rates are rising faster than long-term rates.

beneficiary   The recipient of benefits or funds under a will or other contract; for example, an insurance policy, an annuity, or an Individual Retirement Account (IRA).

bond credit rating   The formal evaluation and analysis that describes the quality of the bonds in a fund's portfolio. Bond credit ratings are typically issued by Standard & Poor's and Moody's Investors Service. Briefly, bonds issued and backed by the federal government are of extremely high quality and are superior to corporate bonds rated AAA, the highest possible rating.

bond fund   A mutual fund that invests in credit instruments; for example, Treasury bonds, mortgage-backed bonds, investment-grade corporate bonds and junk bonds.

book value   The accounting value of a company's stock, which is the amount a shareholder would theoretically receive if the company liquidated its assets. The value is calculated by dividing the net worth of the company by the number of shares outstanding.

broker   An individual or a firm that executes buy and sell orders submitted by another individual.

bullet portfolio strategy   A strategy by which bond maturities are grouped around a single maturity. This is effective when the yield curve is steepening and one maturity is targeted as the ideal place to be on the yield curve.

capital   Money or other assets used to produce income or growth.

capital gain   The margin between the selling price minus the cost basis of an asset.

capital gains distribution   A disbursement to a mutual fund shareholder of gains realized on the sale of fund securities.

capital market   An exchange where debt or equity securities are traded.

cash value   The amount of money that a life insurance policy-holder will receive if he or she allows the policy to lapse or cancels the coverage and surrenders the policy to the insurance company. Also called policyholder's equity, the amount is calculated before adjustment for factors such as policy loans or late premiums. Cash values are a feature of most types of permanent life insurance, such as whole life.

CEO   Chief Executive Officer.

CFO   Chief Financial Officer.

COO   Chief Operating Officer.

common stock   An equity security that represents ownership in a corporation.

convertible security   A security that can be exercised into another security. Examples are bonds, preferred stocks, warrants, and some swap agreements.

cost basis   Used for tax purposes, the cost of an asset, including commissions and other fees, used to determine the gain or loss.

coupon rate   The actual interest rate stated on a bond, typically payable in semiannual installments.

current yield   The interest rate relationship stated as a percent of the annual interest received to the actual market price of the bond.

debt   An amount of money owed from one person or institution to another.

debt to equity ratio   A determination of how much a company has borrowed versus what the company is worth. The measure is calculated by dividing company's debt by its equity.

debt security   A security representing a loan by an investor to an issuer. In return for the loan, the issuer promises to repay the debt on a specified date and to pay interest.

defined benefit plan   A type of pension or retirement plan that has a quantified amount to be paid out annually. Many times, these benefits depend on years of service, age that benefits start, and possible other income constraints. Also, better-than-average investment performance does not increase the level of plan benefits. Compare to defined contribution plan.

defined contribution plan   A type of pension or retirement plan that has a specific amount to be invested annually. Some popular plans are the 401(k) and IRA plans. These plans have no guarantee as to eventual value or benefits. Poor, moderate, or better-than-average investment performance directly impacts the value of the account and potential benefits. Compare to defined benefit plan.

deflation   The economic and financial phenomenon that represents declining prices for goods and services. It is brought on by a decrease in the amount of money in circulation or by a decrease in spending levels.

diversification   The strategy of spreading investments among a number of different securities in order to reduce the risks of investing.

dividend   A distribution of a corporation's profits, which can be in the form of cash or securities.

dividend yield   The current, annualized rate of dividends paid on a share of stocks, divided by its current share price. For a mutual fund, the dividend yield is generally the weighted average yield for stocks it holds as of the profile processing date.

dollar-cost averaging   The practice of purchasing a certain investment at regular intervals regardless of whether the market is moving up or down.

Dow Jones Industrial Average (DJIA)   An average of 30 industrial companies that are representative of the market as a whole. When people say "The market is up 10 points," or "The Dow is doing well," they are usually referring to the DJIA.

durable power of attorney   A written legal document that allows an individual to designate another person to act on his or her behalf, typically in the event the individual becomes disabled or incapacitated.

durable power of attorney for health care   A written legal document that grants another person the authority to act on an individual's behalf with regard to his or her health care decisions.

EAFE (or MSCI EAFE)   Morgan Stanley's Europe, Australia, Far East index. Reflects a widely followed list of stocks from 20 countries.

EPS Growth   A calculation of a company's earnings divided by the number of common shares outstanding. This rate is derived by using a weighted average of the individual EPS growth rates for each company in the portfolio. The one-year EPS growth rate indicates whether a fund is growing more quickly or slowing down.

emerging markets   A broad category of countries that are developing their financial markets and economic infrastructures.

equity   The market value of a security.

equity security   Ownership interest in a company's common and preferred stock.

estate   One's possessions, including owned property and assets.

estate planning   The process by which an individual or company provides for a structure to pass assets upon death. This process typically involves a desire to minimize taxes and preserve the estate. An estate lawyer is highly recommended for expert counsel.

estate tax   A levy imposed by federal and state government upon the death of an individual, subject to applicable exemption amounts.

exchange   An organization, association, or group that maintains or provides a marketplace in which securities can be bought and sold.

executor   A person named in a will to manage an estate. Responsibilities typically include collecting property, paying debts, and distributing assets according to the will.

face value   The stated principal amount of a debt instrument.

fiduciary   A person or institution legally responsible for managing, investing, and distributing funds.

grantor   A person who transfers assets into a trust for another's benefit.

gross estate   The total property or assets held by an individual.

growth fund   A mutual fund that invests in stocks of companies that are expected to experience above-average growth rates. These funds typically have above-average price/earning ratios compared with their equity universe.

guardian   The person legally entrusted with the care of a minor child.

health care proxy   A legal document that designates and authorizes an agent to make decisions regarding medical treatment on behalf of another person only when that person becomes temporarily or permanently incapable of communicating his or her own care or treatment wishes. It can be revoked at any time.

home care agency   A public or private agency that specializes in providing care in the home. Services may include skilled nursing, supportive and personal care, and housekeeping, as well as therapeutic services such as physical therapy.

incapacity   The lack of ability to act on one's own behalf.

index   Statistic by which to measure market performance. *See Standard & Poor's Index.*

Individual Retirement Account (IRA)   A type of personal retirement account. Subject to limits, IRA contributions are deductible against income earned that year. Interest and profits accumulate tax-deferred and the funds can be withdrawn at age 59½ or later. Early withdrawals are subject to a 10% penalty, and withdrawals must begin at 70½. Participants should seek expert counsel on methods of withdrawal.

inflation   A measurement of the rise in prices of goods and services. When prices in general rise, purchasing power subsequently falls.

interest   The charge for the privilege of borrowing money, typically expressed as an annual percentage rate. Also refers to the amount of ownership a stockholder has in a company, usually expressed as a percentage.

inter vivos   Latin term meaning "during the lifetime of." Usually referred to in trusts or other transfers. An inter vivos trust is also called a living trust.

intestate   Having made no legal will.

irrevocable   Unable to be changed or terminated.

joint tenants in common   The type of ownership in which individuals typically own an equal portion.

joint tenancy with right of survivorship   The form of ownership of property that, upon death, will pass directly to another owner regardless of the estate plans in the will.

junk bonds   Noninvestment-grade debt securities. Sometimes called high-yield securities, these securities have bond credit ratings below Baa/BBB−.

Know Your Customer   A concept both stated and implied by various securities regulatory bodies regarding suitability of investments for customers. Article 3 of the Rules of Fair Practice of the National Association of Securities Dealers is typical: "In recommending to a customer the purchase, sale or exchange of any security, a member shall have reasonable grounds for believing that the recommendation is suitable for such customer upon the basis of the facts, if any, disclosed by such customer as to his other security holdings and as to his financial situation and needs." In order to complete the proposed financial plan, financial advisors need to thoroughly know their customers.

ladder portfolio strategy   A strategy that staggers bond maturities so they occur at regular intervals. This is particularly effective during periods of rising interest rates.

life insurance   Insurance that provides protection against the economic loss caused by the death of the insured person.

living trust   A revocable trust established by a grantor during his or her lifetime in which the grantor transfers some or all of his or her property into the trust.

living will   A legal document directing that the maker's or signer's life is not to be artificially supported in the event of a terminal illness or accident.

long-term care insurance   A policy designed to help alleviate some of the costs of long-term care. Benefits are often paid in the form of a fixed dollar amount per day or per visit for covered

LTC expenses and may exclude or limit certain conditions from coverage.

marital deduction   A deduction allowing for the unlimited transfer of any or all property from one spouse to the other, generally free of estate and gift tax.

maturity   The end of the life of a security.

money-market fund   A mutual fund that invests in short-term instruments such as Treasury bills, commercial paper, and asset-backed securities (ABS). These funds try to keep the average maturity or quantitative duration within 2 to 3 months. Also, these funds try to maintain a net asset value (NAV) of $1 per share. However this price level is not guaranteed, and there have been cases where it was broken.

municipal bond   A debt security issued by a state, a municipality, or another subdivision, such as a school, hospital, sewer, or other taxing district, to raise money for infrastructure and other capital expenditures.

mutual fund   A company that combines investors' money and, generally, purchases stocks and/or bonds.

net asset value (NAV)   The market value of mutual fund shares, calculated each business day, by adding up the value of all the securities in the fund's portfolio, subtracting expenses, and dividing this sum by the number of shares outstanding.

nursing home   A residence for persons who need some level of medical assistance and/or assistance with activities of daily living. Not all nursing homes are Medicare-approved/certified facilities.

online trading   Investment activity that takes place over the Internet without the physical inclusion of a broker. Orders are entered via terminals, and reports are returned to the investor in a similar fashion. Confirmations remain a part of the investment or trading process.

option   A privilege sold by one party to another that offers the buyer the right to buy (call) or sell (put) a security at an agreed-upon price during a certain period of time or on a specific date. This type of derivative contract is highly speculative and risky.

penny stock   A low-priced stock, not traded on any exchange, typically trading below $5 per share.

pension   A sum of money paid regularly as a retirement benefit.

policy   A written document that serves as evidence of an insurance contract and contains the pertinent facts about the policyholder the insurance coverage, the insured, and the insurer.

policyholder's equity   *See cash value.*

portfolio   The aggregate investable assets of an individual or institution.

power of attorney   The granting of decision-making authority by one party to another. The amount of authority may be limited or full.

preferred stock   An equity security that has priority relative to ordinary common-stock shares for dividends and return of par amount in the event of a corporate dissolution. Preferred shares can have convertible, cumulative, participating, voting, or other special features.

premium   The payment, or one of a series of payments, the insurer requires to put an insurance policy in force and keep it in force.

price to earnings ratio (P/E ratio)   A measure of how much a company earns in relation to its total stock price. The P/E ratio is calculated by dividing the current price of the stock by its trading 12-months' earnings per share. A higher multiple means investors have higher expectations for future growth and have bid up the stock's price.

Example: Assume ABC Co. sells for $40 per share and has earned $4 per share this year:

$$\frac{\$40}{\$4} = 10 \text{ or } \$40 = 10 \text{ times } \$4.00$$

ABC stock sells for 10 times earnings.

probate   The review or testing of a will before a court of law to ensure its authenticity. Common concerns about the process include time delay in distributing the estate, cost to the estate, and public nature of the process.

professional management   The discipline applied to structuring investment portfolios by those with the required education and experience.

pump and dump   The unscrupulous attempt to attract new buyers of a security by creating the illusion of high trading volume by inflating or pumping up the market for the security, engineering a brief period of inflated prices. Today's Internet trading environment can cause problems for more traders who take advice from bulletin boards, not professionals. These activities may prompt people to purchase securities only to have another individual dump many shares on the marketplace at the momentarily higher prices. This triggers a rapid decline in values and impacts the recent investors.

registered representative   An account executive or broker.

return   The gain or loss for a security in a particular period.

revocable   Able to be changed or terminated.

risk   The variability inherent in investment, speculative, or trading activities. The greater the variability, the higher the risk. Risk can be attributed to many factors, including but not limited to credit, liquidity, market, and currency inflation.

Roth IRA   A retirement account created by the Taxpayer Relief Act of 1997. It is established with after-tax dollars but enjoys the benefits of nontaxable growth and nontaxable withdrawals. These nontaxable withdrawals are subject to certain criteria. Unlike an ordinary IRA account, the Roth IRA does not require minimum distributions at a specified age. Also, there may be favorable tax treatment for estate purposes.

security A financial asset that can be assigned a value and sold. Includes notes, stocks, Treasury stocks, bonds, debentures, certificates of interest, and certificates of participation in a profit-sharing agreement or in a firm.

Series 7 A general securities registered representative license, entitling the holder to sell all types of securities products with the exception of commodities/futures.

SIPC Securities Investor Protection Corporation. An institution created to protect the clients of a securities firm in the event that the firm files for bankruptcy.

skilled nursing facility A Medicare-approved facility staffed and equipped to furnish skilled nursing care and skilled rehabilitation services for which Medicare pays benefits.

Social Security A U.S. federal government program that provides retirement income, health care for the aged, and disability coverage for eligible workers and their dependents.

specialists Securities firms that hold seats on national securities exchanges and are charged with maintaining orderly markets in the securities in which they have exclusive franchises. They buy securities from investors who want to sell and sell when investors want to buy.

Standard & Poor's 500 Index A popular index that incorporates a broad base of 500 stocks, chosen for market size, liquidity, and industry group representation. It is widely considered to be the benchmark for large stock investors. Some of the stocks have a greater influence on the direction of the market than others, so the S&P 500 is calculated by giving a greater weight to some stocks, according to market capitalization.

stock symbol A unique letter symbol assigned to a security. For U.S. securities, one- two- and three-letter symbols indicate that the security is listed and trades on an exchange. NASDAQ-traded securities have a unique four- or five-letter symbol assigned.

street name The term to indicate a security is held in the name of a brokerage firm rather than in the customer's name.

tax-deferred   A situation or an investment whereby the tax liability is delayed. Examples include retirement plans such as 401(k) plans, IRAs, and annuities.

term insurance   A life insurance benefit payable only if the insured dies during a specified period. This type of policy typically carries no cash value.

testamentary trust   A trust created upon an individual's death following the terms of his or her will.

total return   The aggregate value of share price appreciation, dividends, and interest.

Treasury bill   Also known as a T-bill, a marketable U.S. government debt security with a maturity of less than one year.

Treasury bond   Also known as a T-bond, a marketable, fixed-interest U.S. government debt security with a maturity of more than ten years.

Treasury note   Also known as a T-note, a marketable, fixed-interest U.S. government debt security with a maturity of between one and ten years.

trust   A written legal document a grantor creates during his or her lifetime, or at death, for the benefit of another.

trustee   The person a trust document names who will manage the property the trust owns and distribute any income according to the document. A trustee can be an individual or a corporate fiduciary.

UGMA   Uniform Gift to Minors Act. An irrevocable gift of securities to a minor. The securities are registered in the name of an adult who is the child's custodian. The funds pass to the child at his or her age of majority.

uncertainty   Risk or volatility.

value fund   A mutual fund that invests in undervalued companies. These companies may exhibit lower-than-average ratios, such as price/earnings, price/sales, or book value. Nevertheless, these stocks are viewed by participants as being bargain-priced or value-attractive.

variable annuity   An annuity policy in which the underlying investments are not guaranteed. Performance is dependent on the total return of the underlying mutual funds chosen by the investor.

whole life insurance   A policy that remains in force throughout the insured's lifetime, provided premiums are paid as specified in the policy. Whole life insurance also builds a savings element (*see cash value*) as the level of the premium approaches the level of the death benefit.

will   A legal document directing the disposal of one's property after one's death.

yield   The rate of return, usually dividend or interest payments, on an investment. Expressed as a percentage of market price.

yield curve   The relationship between a bond's risk and its return at a specific time, expressed in graphic form. The most typical yield curve shows the range of yields from a 3-month Treasury bill to a 30-year Treasury bond. A positive yield curve happens when short-term interest rates are lower than long-term interest rates. A negative or inverted yield curve takes place when short-term interest rates are higher than long-term interest rates. When short-term and long-term interest rates are equal, this is a flat yield curve.

zero-coupon bond   A bond that makes no periodic interest payments, but instead is sold at a deep discount from its face value. The owner of the bond receives the return by the gradual appreciation of the security until maturity at face value.

Index

Praise for *WealthBuilding*

"An excellent readable text, especially in these volatile times. Should be required reading for those who wish to enhance their wealth for their retirement years."

—A.L. Horvath, Retired Vice President, GE

"Real life case studies and step-by-step guidance provide the common sense knowledge that will help you make the most of your retirement and estate planning. Now that I've read it, I'm making sure my children read it."

—Ken Swimm, Retired President,
Lockheed Martin Management and Data Systems Co.

"I have worked closely with David Reiser and Robert DiColo over the past 15 years in helping clients reach their goals. In some cases they have been an integral part of my COO team; in other cases I have been an integral part of their COO team. *WealthBuilding* clearly defines the issues, the pitfalls, and solutions to creating and implementing a successful financial plan. It should be required reading for those seriously interested in securing their financial future."

—Grafton H. "Cap" Willey, IV, Managing Partner,
Rooney, Plotkin & Willey, LLP, Certified Public Accountants/
Board Member, National Small Business United (NSBU)

About the Wealth Stories in This Book

The Wealth Stories referenced in this book are adapted from the experiences that the authors have had in addressing and serving the needs of various clients. For the purposes of privacy and confidentiality, however, certain specific circumstances regarding the clients' financial matters and the planning related thereto have been modified accordingly.